It Can
Be Done

The Real Heroes
of the Inner City

Fred Catherwood

The Lutterworth Press

Cambridge

First Published in 2000 by:
The Lutterworth Press
P.O. Box 60
Cambridge
CB1 2NT
England

e-mail: **publishing@lutterworth.com**
website: **http://www.lutterworth.com**

ISBN 0 7188 3003 2

British Library Cataloguing in Publication Data:
A catalogue record is available from the British Library.

© Fred Catherwood, 2000

Printed in England by
Redwood Books

Contents

Introduction

This book is a story of a fight for the soul of our country. Most of us today go with the flow and seldom feel the strength of the currents which are sweeping British society. Maybe that is changing. The Centre for Policy Studies recently published a piece by David Shelbourne:

> Is it an old moral thing or a new moral thing that there is now an arson attack in at least three schools every day? Or that 86% of alarm calls in the Metropolitan Police area are false? Or that trees and shrubs planted in memory of the Dunblane victims were stolen within days from the local cemetery?
>
> Has there ever been such violence directed in time of peace by youth against the frailest and most elderly, so that even women in their eighties come to be raped? Is it old thing or a new that doctors – a thousand of whom are assaulted every year – and teachers should feel themselves at risk from those for whom they care? When, before, could nursing be considered Britain's "most dangerous profession," with one nurse in three, compared with one policeman in four, suffering an act of violence in accident and emergency units?
>
> And yet there are, everywhere, evasions. These seek to show, and have us believe that nothing can any longer be done about our moral condition, or that nothing needs to be done about it, since nothing much is at fault with it in the first place.
>
> The cumulative effect of these evasions is often to paralyse the debate itself. And when all other arguments fail, the objector is dismissed as a 'moral authoritarian.'
>
> There has not, since the French Revolution, been a greater concern for and insistence upon the promotion and expansion of individual rights in an already deeply free society. Yet this culture of rights coexists with a cynicism with the distinction between right and wrong. There seems no doubt about the former and every doubt, assiduously promoted, about the latter.

This book aims to show that we should not throw up our hands and that, as its title asserts, we can all do something about it. Its heroes are an army of volunteers, working in sectors of our society which the welfare state does not cover. They fight day after day to rescue the victims of the social disaster which, as David Shelbourne argues, threatens immense damage to the structure of British society.

These volunteers are out among the gangs of fatherless children in the no-go housing estates . They take teenagers off the streets and help them find homes, training and jobs. They sort out the debts of single mothers, compound with their creditors and find cookers and beds to replace those the bailiffs have removed. They help prisoners to keep in touch with their families and ex-prisoners to come off drugs and find steady jobs. They do the shopping for those dying of AIDS and clean their houses; they find safe space for separated parents to hand over custody of their children to each other; they try to mend marriages, look after latch-key kids, help children who live in cramped and noisy homes with their homework, counsel those who are confused and depressed by our disordered society, give advice to pregnant teenagers and support to abandoned wives and mothers.

They did not expect to be called upon to deal with this tidal wave of trouble. For nearly forty years Britain relied on a full employment policy to keep people at work, and on the social services of a well-funded welfare state to look after those in need. But now all that has changed.

The full employment policy was abandoned in the early eighties when unemployment rose to three and a half million, far higher than in the great slump of the 1930s. The loss of tax revenue from employment, added to the huge increase in unemployment benefits, put burdens on the British budget and cash constraints on the social services from which they have never recovered. As if that were not enough, taxes on the incomes of those who had jobs were reduced and taxes on everyone's spending increased.

The rich got much richer, the poor got steadily poorer and those leaving school at sixteen and unable to find a job were refused any benefit from social services. It did not help teenagers in high rise estates among the new industrial wastelands suffering 50% unemployment to be told curtly and coldly, 'Get on your bike.'

Had family solidarity held firm, as it did in the slump of the 1930s, the teenagers would not have found themselves out on the streets. They might even have had the money for a bike. But the major result of the permissive legislation of the late 1960s was a large-scale breakup of the family, with a severe knock-on effect on all the children. When a marriage came apart, rows began between mum's new man and the stroppy teen-ager who had left school, couldn't find a job and, with no benefit income, still needed to be fed and housed. Teenage boys on the streets or in squats with their mates said that anything was better than living with the aggro at home. And girls, who had left home because they were being abused, were picked up by the pimps and suffered far worse abuse.

It was this horde of homeless teenagers which first warned the churches that the social services could no longer cope. Together with those returned from mental institutions to a 'community' which no longer existed, they began to knock on church doors, the age-old place of refuge for those in need. At first, the churches, not realising that the need was getting greater while social funding was getting less, tried to send them back to the social services.

The minister of a Pentecostal church down by Aberdeen docks told us,

They started coming every Sunday night and I kept on telling them that it was not my job and they should go to the welfare. They said that the welfare could not help them and I thought they were just not trying hard enough. Then one night a boy slipped past me into the church and we couldn't find him anywhere and couldn't close up until we did find him. At last we discovered him under the desk in the vestry. He pleaded with us desperately not to send him away because he had nowhere else to go and, at last, I thought that maybe this really was the voice of God speaking to me.

So the church decided to clear their dockside cellars, they put in a gas ring, kettles and crockery, toilets, wash-basins and some old armchairs, making a refuge with a door on to the dock side, open from eight in the evening to eight in the morning, and became part of the new volunteer army which is now filling the yawning gaps in the welfare state. The little minister would have been no match for the rougher types, but they found an amiable, fair-haired, warden, six feet tall, broad and strong who said with a smile, 'If there's trrouble, I chust thrrow them oot!'

Every year brings new needs, new projects and more experience. The rising need has also brought stronger personal commitment from the volunteers and has forced them to learn faster. New projects have no staff manual, because the social experiment of the permissive society and the collapse of the family, our basic social institution, is unprecedented. And yet, just as society is becoming more fragmented, our singleminded drive for more wealth has made us totally dependent on the integrity of high technology systems, on last minute distribution systems which depend on unblocked highways and round the clock access to the huge assembly plants and the supermarkets. To add riches to riches we have killed off the local independent manufacturer and local retail store, and made ourselves far more dependent on each other than ever before.

So what has gone wrong?

In 1997 a report was published by the Evangelical Alliance based on replies from 70 social projects, who gave their views on the underlying causes of their clients' problems. The consistent reply was that the two root problems were persistent high unemployment and the breakup of the family and that there was a malign interaction between these two problems. Teenagers holding jobs which brought a steady income into the family would not have been so readily thrown out on to the streets and had the family held together, as it did in the 1930s, parents would have encouraged the young to stick at school and learn a trade, so parental unemployment would not have had such dire side-effects.

But on current trends, this malign interaction is likely to get much worse. The number of broken families increases with each new generation and the tendency of unrestricted world capital markets to shattering collapse is likely to make full employment more difficult, unless governments can show unusual speed in changing course. But, among voters, the milk of human kindness has been curdled by the determination to hold on to every last penny, whatever the needs of our poorer neighbours.

So, if the voluntary sector is to bridge the rapidly widening gap between need and provision for help, they have to learn from each other as fast as possible how they can use limited resources to maximum effect. The greater part of this book aims to help that practical process by showing how some of the front-runners have done it.

The last two chapters look at the duty of both church and state to look after those in need. In the parable of the Good Samaritan and in his own care for the sick and hungry, Christ makes the duty of his followers crystal clear. He teaches that, in the final judgement, it is those who feed the hungry, give water to the thirsty, visit the sick and the prisoner who will be rewarded and those who do not, though they call themselves Christian, will be condemned. 'Faith without works is dead.'

Half a century of the welfare state may have atrophied the Christian duty of care, but the church is not a cosy club for like-minded people, dedicated, like the Pharisees, to keeping the sinful world from coming through the door. The Christian church is a caring and helpful part of society or it is nothing. From the beginning of our history, when the early monasteries looked after the needs of those around them, down to Barnardo's Homes and the Salvation Army, the Christian church and its institutions have been a place of refuge for the needy. It is this Christian care in a brutal world which converted the Roman Empire and, after it fell, the Goths, the Franks and Saxons, the Danes and the Slavs, until the church spread right across Europe.

Christians believe that both church and state are separately ordained by God for the good of all people. They have different functions, officers, and sanctions, but both state and church are under the same moral law. Neither should dominate the other and both should be mutually support- ive. The church should not take the sword or use the power of the state to coerce and the state should not undermine the moral law, as it has done for the last thirty years, with disastrous results.

'I don't know what these people teach, but I know what they have done for our old folk and for our kids, so I'm here to find out.'

Today it is not considered politically correct to take special notice of the Christian church. Current social theory is that we are a multi-faith society where the Christian church is simply one faith among many and has no special right to be heard. But if that were really the governing principle, then government should listen to the high view of the family which Christians, Jews, Muslims, Sikhs and Hindus - and indeed Buddhists, Confucians and Shinto - all hold in common.

The truth is that secular humanism has an agenda on the family which respects the views of none of those faiths. But, unlike the historic faiths, which have a written body of belief, tested in the crucible of real life over the centuries, secular humanism is a huge experiment with no agreed body of belief, no culture of acceptable behaviour and certainly no record over long centuries in containing the worse side of human nature.

The primary argument of this book is that the church has to earn respect for its views by the Christian love which it shows for its needy neighbours, parish by parish, ward by ward, and city by city. That should give decisive reinforcement to the argument for a Christian basis for British law and culture and for the traditional partnership between church and state, which recognises their mutual interests in promoting good and discouraging evil.

The central stories of this book show that, down at the grass roots, the theoretical arguments against partnership between church and state give way when dealing with the stark realities of social collapse. Local government and local church simply get on with the job, especially where the churches work together. It is hard for local government to argue that the church should not try to establish a degree of moral order in people's lives which would make the community safer and encourage productive citizens. The police can only begin to keep order only when the great majority of society accepts that violence and robbery are morally wrong and not just illegal.

The Christian church has shown that it can help to deliver a moral order. It is still organised and articulate and it is everywhere. The reason why Christians around the world argue so strongly for freedom of speech is that in an open market of ideas, they have the strongest record of success. The most disastrous periods in the Christian church have been the centuries where the political class have taken over the powerful offices of the church and, in the spirit of Antichrist, imposed their own ideas. The essence of totalitarianism is that the political class should decide not just what is legal and illegal, but also what is right and wrong. Political correctness had a long and oppressive history even before anyone thought of Fascism or Communism.

1

The Breakup of the Family

Disoriented families

'Well he laid me out with a machete, didn't he.' She was a pretty dark-haired girl of nineteen, with a child tucked under her arm, one of the three remaining from the three pairs of twins she had borne. We had asked her what had forced her to leave home.

She said that a neighbour had attacked her because he thought that she had been spying on him while he was breaking into a house opposite.

'He said he's seen the curtains part. But it wasn't me watching him, it was the wind.' He didn't believe her and after he had attacked her, she had to hide in a succession of squats before 'Save the Family' gave her and her children refuge in their large farm house, Plas Bellin in Flintshire.

Edna Speed, who founded 'Save the Family' as a place for the homeless and needy, had been head teacher some years ago in a nursery school in the Lache estate on the outskirts of Chester. She found that the culture on the estate made education almost irrelevant. On Monday mornings the children would queue to get into the school because they were cold, frightened and famished. It was the only safe, warm place they knew and the only place where they could find any breakfast.

The school was also the only statutory body on an estate of six thousand people. There were no police, no probation officers, no social services and no housing authority – just the school. It was known to be an estate of undiluted problems. Many children who suffered abuse were sent into care and, when they came out of care, they couldn't find their family, which, as likely as not, had split and split again. They were described as 'emotional cripples', who would never recover without help. Before the children could begin to learn, their parents' problems had to be tackled.

Children came to the school without enough clothing, shuffling in in slippers. The school organised appeals for clothes and for logs for fires. One winter, when there was a big freeze-up, the school gave warm meals to a large part of the neighbourhood and it was hard to persuade the children to go home. The teachers were the first people who had ever shown interest in them. There were eighteen year-old mothers with black eyes, three children and no family to help them. Often they had been kept up all night with police raids or had slept in the cold because their electricity had been turned off. The school was the only place to which they could look for help, for hot porridge, for blankets and for transport to hospital. The social workers were all from outside the estate.

A supporter bought a minibus for the school, which also helped with trips to the shops, to hospital and for prison visits to places they had never even heard of – "What is Scotland?" And they had no idea of times – "Thursday?" It was impossible to convey to the local politicians the depths of the problems.

The staff of the school and the churches in Chester established a 'Sunday School' in the school on Monday nights and one to two hundred came, including parents. Then they started a Sunday afternoon service and they all came to that too. Many workers at the refuge today have come from the Sunday School – and were among some of the toughest cases. And yet they were the foundation stones of 'Save the Family.'

Edna Speed's right hand is Val Trice. She used to work in a Methodist Church in Wrexham as a drug and alcohol rehabilitation counsellor and is now the manager of Plas Bellin, the larger of 'Save the Family's' two hostels. Her husband looks after the two vans, the heating and electrics and anything else that needs fixing.

This kind of project starts, as 'Save the Family' did, just by meeting some pressing need. As well as helping parents on the estate, Edna Speed and her husband started to take families away from the estate on outings and short holidays. On one such holiday, a young woman came with all she owned in a pile of black bin bags. Her drunken husband had completely demolished their home on the Lache estate. Furniture had been reduced to firewood and gas fire and cooker ripped from their sockets, light fittings smashed and the bath, wash basin and mirror were a pile of sharp pieces of crockery. The family were evicted, and she and the children began a nomadic life at aid hostels.

That made Edna Speed wonder whether she could find a centre which would give such families a place of refuge and safety, where their lives could be put back together again and where they could get into the rhythm of tackling the practical problems of life, shopping, paying the bills and getting the children to school.

It was just then that Plas Bellin came on to the market, with eleven bedrooms, barns, sheds and ten acres of woodland and at a bargain price of £65,000. But it had been badly vandalised and the cost of repair was uncertain. Eventually the Council offered free labour for the repairs under the Manpower Services Commission scheme. That took three years and, when completed, the surveyors declared the work a 'dreadful bodge-up.' To get that put right took another two years of legal argument, ending in a lease from the Coal Board who owned it. Anyone with less tenacity and determination would have given up long before.

Even that was not the end. The Coal Board was privatised and the next owner pressed them to buy at a price they couldn't possibly afford. But Edna Speed and her husband prayed, and so did the church. She also badgered everyone who had any influence and at last she had an afford-able deal.

In the eleven years since it was opened 'Save the Family' has looked after well over two thousand people.

The problem that has faced most of those who come to them and want to start a normal productive life is that none of the government training courses start at their level. The nearest is 'pre-vocational and special needs training' but even this is 'a million miles away' from the needs of many of them.

To begin to benefit from this basic government course, they have to make the transition from homelessness, long-term unemployment, poverty, sexual and physical abuse, lack of self-confidence and a feeling of worth-lessness. Some have a record of drug-abuse, some a criminal record and some nervous and mental health problems. But the project finds that, with time (which means money) and patience the transition can be made.

The work starts with training on basic life-skills, such as personal hygiene, proper dress and punctuality, and then goes on to look at previous job experience and at their abilities and skills; then to prepare them for the 'Pre-vocational training.' They find that each person needs to have an action plan within an acceptable time-frame, agreed and signed by them and by their trainer. The trainers are funded by charitable trusts and work in conjunction with the local TEC.

At the time of writing there are fifty children there, many of whom had never been to school. One three year old was recently sent away from school after three hours of nursery schooling because, no doubt doing what he saw others do at home, he had attacked the teacher with scissors.

All children of school age are taken to school every day and the work-ers help the parents with their problems in bringing them up and try to help them to introduce a family routine – getting up and going to bed at set times is the most basic.

Even if there had not been the appalling cases of abuse in care in North Wales, Edna Speed feels that the official remedy of sending children into care violates the natural process and gives the children no role model. So she tries to keep families together. She thinks that social workers do what they can, but they are only able to get snapshots. The sources of the troubles they see are deep and complex. They need continuous attention over a period of time, and there is probably no area of the lives of their clients that is right. She says,

Their whole lives are out of gear and their only expertise is in outwitting authority. They have to be taught that it is not normal for children to break windows. So the job needs a strong sense of humour!

The most vivid memory I have of our first visit to Plas Bellin is the rush of children to gather round Edna Speed when we walked with her out of the front door. They wanted to show her everything and to talk about everything. It was clear that for those who had not known much love, she was love personified. One warm supporter said,

> They have discovered something here which most of us take for granted: security, relationships and someone to whom to spill out their troubles. It's probably the closest some have known to a real home.

The girl who was laid out by the machete said, 'I had a feeling that God loved me through it all.' She wrote a hymn,

> In everything you hope or do
> I'll encourage and believe in you.
> Your every joy is my joy too.
> You'll always have my love.
>
> No matter what, no matter where,
> You count on me and I'll be there,
> To understand, to show I care,
> You'll always have my love.
>
> When we asked her what inspired her, she said,
> 'Well I was at the Sunday School wasn't I?'

Where secular society has failed, it can hardly complain if Christians who step into the breach try to help those who have lost their way by giving them the signposts which Christians themselves have learnt to use and trust.

The Lache estate is not alone in its poverty, and unemployment has something to do with it. Plas Bellin takes families from the Welsh side of the Dee where, until the 1980s there was a flourishing steel industry. But the Shotton steel works had to be closed in the early eighties because the artificially high pound produced by a monetarist government made it unprofitable.

All over Britain there are similar estates which have lost their basic source of income and the hope of a job which makes it worth staying at school and learning a trade. But as hope evaporates, so does ambition and effort. And with nothing to do and all day to hang around, it is small wonder that the young get into trouble.

It was not always like that. In the 1960s and 1970s my jobs in public service probably took me round more shop floors than most people. In my last job as Chairman of the British Overseas Trade Board, we started our series of sixteen major export conferences in Sheffield. The great Cutler's Hall was packed with exporters and their shop stewards (one of whom, Dick Caborn, is now a Minister) to study the success stories of four Sheffield exporters which we had visited the day before. In those days the city was famous for its successful, internationally competitive, specialist steel mills. Today it is famous for 'The Full Monty,' its opening sequence in a derelict factory, its heroes the redundant workers.

In nearby Barnsley, the main employer, the coal industry, has gone. But with a policy of full employment, there would have been enough demand in the economy to diversify and plant new industry. But in big bleak estates in Sheffield, Barnsley, Glasgow, Edinburgh and all the great cities of England, Scotland, Wales and Northern Ireland, youth unemployment is high, usually over 50%.

Today they are written out of the script as 'sink estates' as if somehow they contained another species of being about whom there was little anyone could do. But to Edna Speed and those like her each person, however far gone, is a special human being, made in the image of God. As a Christian she believes that they are not out of God's script, so they cannot be out of hers. And where the world gives up, she fights on. She says, 'It's a country away from its God, left to the tender mercies of the wicked.'

The problem, as she sees it, is that the culture of children who do not know their mothers or fathers is so alien to ordered life that the government cannot tackle it. But she says that God can touch them.

What comes through as you talk to her is her passion to help put right what has gone wrong, her feeling that, among the people around her, she and her team are all that stands for hope and against despair. It is that passion which has enabled her to overcome one insuperable obstacle after another. Against indifferent officials and distant London bureaucrats she has marshalled MPs, Bishops and all the good and the great she could lay hands on and has pushed them into the battle on behalf of the poor and needy. When I told one of them that I'd met her, he said wryly, 'So she's got at you too!'

She probably does not see herself as a leader, just as someone who happened to be there, the head teacher of a nursery school, who could help when there seemed to be no one else. And she certainly does not see herself as a one-woman band. 'Save the Family' is now a team with competent professionals. Val Trice is in charge on the larger site at Plas Bellin, sitting behind her desk in a small room and dealing plainly and bluntly with every plausible excuse that slips around the door. There is an office in Chester with a full-time resource administrator and also a place where people in need in the city can come for help.

The project has between twenty-four and thirty staff, with six to eight on duty at any time during the day and two on duty overnight. The cost of the project is £1,100 a day, of which about £550 comes from housing benefit. A resettlement officer is funded by the Department of the Environment. About £450 a day comes from Trusts and business and most of the balance from a few faithful churches. The fund-raising is done by one full-time worker, and the work is managed from the Chester office. Edna Speed also spends a good deal of time in giving presentations to churches and business groups such as Rotary Clubs.

The liaison with the Social Services seems good. They refer people in need to 'Save the Family' and are in continuous contact on the details of their cases. It is not the fault of those who run the Social Services that they are so stretched, or that they cannot always fulfil their statutory obligations.

Nor can the Social Services deal with the moral issues which people in trouble need to face. Today's doctrine is that the Christian faith can have no special place in a multi-faith society. But those who get blind drunk and smash up their homes are not going to be put right by the doctrines of political correctness. So 'Save the Family' is based on the Christian faith, and transports people from the estates to a Sunday service in Plas Bellin's chapel. It is their faith that drives those who are trying to help, and, as they see it, it is the power behind the dramatic changes in so many lives. They are doing what no one else seems able to do, so no one can really complain about the Christian belief which motivates them, the belief that no one is irredeemable.

Drugs in the family

At the back entrance to the shopping centre a schoolgirl was screaming at a boy of about twenty, 'You have no right to push it, you shouldn't do it.'

He had an apologetic smile on his face, 'I don't push it, they want it.'

As I walked past, her noisy protests went on. About twenty minutes later, as I came out, a group of youths were gathered round, one with a mobile phone. A car drew up, money was passed in and something else passed out.

Every parent must feel the same as the older sister. Drugs depersonalise those who take them. They move out of their normal social relationships into a fantasy world of their own and no longer relate to those around them. And, of course that's only the beginning. Illegal drugs are highly addictive and those who want to give them up are gripped by a force which overpowers both logic and will.

Despite the predictable results, there are those who favour legalisation of, at least, some drugs. I once visited a detoxification centre in my constituency. They found that, though they could get people off drugs, they could not keep them off. They argued that by putting drugs outside the law, we created a whole criminal underworld, flush with enough money to bribe not only police, but also whole governments. These are strong arguments and we may hear more of them, but there are even more powerful arguments the other way.

Christians believe that we are responsible for our relationships with our families, our neighbours and our colleagues and must not wipe out our ability to keep to our social obligations. At some level of drug penetration it would be impossible to run our highly interdependent industrial society. The millennium bug would be nothing to the damage that could be done by airline pilots, or operators in food-processing plants, high on drugs, which are not so easily detected as alcohol and which cause addiction much more quickly.

There is damage enough already from a drugs culture that is widespread among the young of all classes.

Leigh's family were professional middle class. But his father left his mother, his dog died and he failed his O-levels. Someone gave him cannabis and 'I got accepted into a crowd which had given up. I didn't have to prove anything to these people. At home I was getting into loud music, I was rebelling, taking anything I could inject. It was fun. It happened so quickly.'

After arguments at home about what he should do after dropping out of school he moved into a squat, feeling that it was the only place where he could come and go. He became dirty and dishevelled. His mother came to the squat and was threatened by someone with a knife.

Soon he was addicted to heroin. He says that he began burgling shops, spent his days in planning how to get drugs and could feel himself becoming paranoid on the drugs. He went to prison for six weeks for hitting someone with a broken bottle and was careless about overdosing, because 'life had no real worth.'

What finally saved him was a meeting, at a point of desperation, with a friend of his mother's who was a Christian and who persuaded him that there was still hope. But he was one of the fortunate ones. Many do not live to tell the tale. Leigh was helped by a Christian rehabilitation centre, Yeldall Manor, near Reading. He has now recovered and has found a job.

Churches hesitate to take on this specialised form of care, and usually the work has been started by projects that found that drug or alcohol addiction was the main problem of those they had taken into their care.

Adullam Homes, whose major work is rehabilitation of ex-prisoners, started drug rehabilitation too.

Claire, aged 18, was referred to them by her drugs worker. She had a history of addiction to speed and ecstasy because she found that both gave her self-confidence. She had been living with her mother, but there was too much drug-taking there, so she moved to a friend's house. Although she had no criminal record, her drug-taking was leading her in that direction, so Adullam found her shared and supported accommodation so that she could keep a drug-free lifestyle until she found somewhere permanent. She had counselling from a drugs worker and gradually her life began to stabilise, until finally she was able to move on.

Drug rehabilitation needs specialist qualifications and experience. A warm heart is needed, but it is not enough. So, in 1992, Adullam Homes went further and opened a 'substance misuse' Rehabilitation Centre, Manna Farm, near Nottingham to accommodate twenty-four residents and with six move-on properties.

Paul Stears, their director, says that a lot of those who come there have become addicted because they feel worthless. Sometimes it is because of rejection by a dysfunctional family or a wife, sometimes because of sexual abuse, and quite often because they have picked up the addiction in prison, where drugs come in hidden in handbags, bras or in books with a hole cut in the pages. Somewhere in the addict's life there is a problem; drugs are the symptom and rehabilitation starts with one to one counselling to find the underlying problem.

Manna Farm has two full-time counsellors who try to help put the addict's life together, to build up their feeling of self-worth, to discover their needs and their skills as well as their qualifications and to help them plan for their future. To begin with, they try to fill their days with activity, house duties and outdoor sports, such as football and skating. Then, after a few months, they try to fix them up with college courses, such as computing, which will help them to find jobs. Local churches find them decorating jobs so that they can build practical skills, and after four months they move out to a safe house rented by Manna Farm, but continue to be under supervision for another four or five months.

Adullam is a Christian organisation and the professional staff are Christians. But they have a firm rule against pressing their Christian faith on those they are trying to help, since they do not want to exploit the vulnerability and dependence of those who need help. But, as Christians who believe in the worth and dignity of every human being, and who have duty of care to those in need, they hope everyone there will see their faith reflected in their lives, and find that those who want to know more will ask. About half the residents go to church on Sunday and the local churches are active in their support of the work.

Paul Stears says that drugs are the centre of the addict's life and that their removal leaves a vacuum crying out to be filled, so they have to try to see that they leave with a focused project to fill the void and give them something creative to do with their lives. A few do become Christians, a few relapse, but, so far as they know, the majority are able to reintegrate into normal life.

Jane Bellamy is one of the counsellors. She says that the age of those coming for help has dropped sharply. Five years ago only one was under twenty, now only one is over thirty and the average age is twenty five.

She finds that the first hurdle is to make them see that the real problem is not so much the drug as the addiction (shown in the increasing frequency of fixes) which takes away their free will and compels them to go on. Then she has to deal with their feeling of complete worthlessness, their conviction that whatever they do nothing will ever go right and, underlying that, their reluctance to take responsibility. 'Life is not brilliant, so why bother?'

She points out to them that the decision to come in for detox and rehab showed that they can be in control. Then she goes through what else they can do and, over time, tries to help them build a vision for the future that is worthwhile and within their grasp. But at the same time she has to prevent their leaning on her and has to encourage them to take the responsibility themselves. As a slimmer doesn't see the difference from day to day, and needs someone else to point it out, so she encourages them to mark their steady progress.

Since drugs have been the answer to the problems of their life and their angry reactions to those problems, she has to show them first of all how to control anger without drugs. Drugs have been the pivot of their lives. The first waking thought has been how to raise the money for a fix. Drugs have taken priority. They have to understand how chemical dependency works and its damaging effect, which throws 'family, friends, partners and jobs all out of the window.' So they must not only turn their back on it but also build a new positive centre for their lives. The outside activities during their eight-month stay are designed to give them the capacity to build another life. They must see something positive in front of them.

Counselling is not straightforward. It has to face the fact that drug addicts have learnt to tell lies, to be manipulative and to make others take responsibility. So one to one counselling has to be backed up by group sessions where they expose each others' cover-ups and force one another to face up to the truth.

The problem of institutional care is cost. The current cost to the social services of sending someone to Manna Farm is £332.50 per week, less whatever the Social Services would otherwise pay in benefits. So, simply because of cost, institutions can only deal with a fraction of the problem, maybe no more than 5%. Residential centres like Manna Farm seem vital for those who are really desperate to get right away from the friends and the dealers who would drag them back into their local drug culture.

A day centre, by contrast, is not only cheaper; it is also better for those who want to come off drugs while having time off from their employment (sometimes the employer gives them long-term sick leave, or holds the job open for them during rehabilitation), or while looking after a young family.

The South Yorkshire Community Church in Sheffield's city centre has a local drug rehabilitation programme, called Kickstart.

Christine Tooze, who is the leader of the team ministry at the church, says that they didn't set out to help drug addicts. The work started as a project for those who were confused and depressed and who dropped in for help and guidance. They found that poor personal relationships were at the heart of most depression and confusion. A lot of relationship problems arise when people have jumped into bed together before they really know each other, and then they wonder why it is not working out. In the past they would have had guidance and advice from parents. But the permissive generation of the 1960s and 1970s had not set them the example of parental skills and had let them do whatever they liked. There were no rules and no boundaries to behaviour. But two people living together have to have some rules, especially about finance.

James and Jenny met at work, decided to live together, and her parents took them in. They had two children, but soon she was demanding that all they had should be split equally and also that she had the freedom to go off with other men. When she left him, he discovered that she taken everything with her, but had only paid half of each bill. So he came to the church in great confusion and distress, wondering what had gone wrong.

The church found that if someone came at this stage, they could help them; but the quickest relief to those with a problem was normally to blot it out with drugs. So soon the church was spending as much or more time in dealing with people who had already taken to drugs and that problem had to be given priority.

Often the first person through the door was a distressed partner or parent, because it was very hard to hold a family together when one member was on drugs. The problem had become so great that the Health and Social Services were overloaded and often waiting lists were shut down or were so long that the drug users had died before they could be seen. Fifty people in their twenties had died in one year.

The hospitals in Sheffield had only five beds for detoxification. It couldn't deal with the state of mind that put them on drugs in the first place, and when they leave they don't stay off. It was especially hard for any who stayed in their own city, full of people who would tempt them back.

So the church opened a full-time day centre for five days a week and the addicts were placed in Christian homes for the period of detoxification, to help them through the difficult period and to try to show them 'what a family was all about'. Afterwards they returned home to face and overcome the temptations and stresses in their own community, while continuing to receive the support and help of the centre. Mothers with children find the programme especially helpful, since, unlike a residential programme, it enables them to return home in the evening to care for their children.

Christine Tooze says that it is easier to relate to drug addicts in pictures and feelings. The drugs give a 'warm' feeling and the family gives an alternative 'warm' feeling, and one that lasts.

She says that the drugs are terribly destructive. Young addicts will do anything to their family to find the money. They will put a knife to their mother's throat. One mother went out to work and came home to a completely bare house. Everything had been sold. Even the fireplace had been ripped out. The addicts themselves say that they are torn apart. Some find hard drugs a terrifying spiritual experience. One addict could not go to sleep because, when he closed his eyes, he saw an evil face, which told him, 'You belong to me and I'm not going to let you go.' He said that he thought it was the devil.

Yet, when off drugs, many of them are talented and creative – but they've never had the opportunity to develop their gifts. One of the reasons why they take to drugs is 'a bad home life, one with no family values and no beliefs'; another is broken relationships. There is also peer pressure among the young especially to experiment on soft drugs like cannabis, and then they often move on to heroin and other substances. 'They think that you can try it and it won't happen to you, so you take a drug three or four times and that's where addiction starts.'

Christine Tooze does not believe that there are any 'soft' drugs. All drugs are mind and mood altering substances and most of those with whom Kickstart has to deal have started on cannabis. Other drugs, such as crack-cocaine, have the effect of making people violent, but they all lower tolerance levels, which explains how so much in the home gets smashed by drug addicts, and how respect for other people vanishes.

She says that addiction affects all classes of people. They recently helped a solicitor, and the son of a police sergeant. About 60% of those who come on the programme are from 19 to 26. The age of first use is now much lower. There are children as young as eleven on heroin. The main problem with young users is unemployment and nothing to do. There is no plan for them, no purpose in their lives and they become very cynical. They don't have a proper relationship with other people, that gets them into rows and makes them look for a way of escape.

She finds, as others elsewhere have found, that those who make a Christian commitment are by far the most likely to stay off drugs. Most of the rest go back. So they offer a process, which begins where they are, but can go on towards a Christian faith which fills the vacuum.

Once through detoxification, they attend a programme from 10 to 4 every day, filling the day with activity, mental and physical. They also take part in a twelve-step programme. The first step is to admit that they have found themselves unmanageable, that they have no power to get themselves out of addiction, and to begin to realise that they must have a commitment to a higher being outside themselves, who has given us rules to live by. They have to recognise that their behaviour has been wrong, that they must make amends to those whom they have damaged. Then, for those who are willing to go on to the next stage, they must allow God to heal them. The next three steps are commitments to specific life patterns and the last two are to maintaining these commitments by reading their bibles and going to church.

At first this Christian input, even though voluntary, worried the authorities, but an independent assessor for Sheffield Health asked clients, 'Have you on any occasion in your time on the programme felt under pressure to adopt Christian values?' and reported, 'All clients answered no.'

Initially two people ran the counselling centre, but it expanded rapidly and now costs £30,000 a year, mainly borne by the church, with the drugs programme costing £154,000, nearly half of which is found externally from trusts and individuals. The counselling staff pass on clients to experts, such as accountants, to sort out financial problems, doctors for medical problems, those expert in dealing with abuse, and in marriage counselling. Clients are expected to pay whatever they can afford, from 15p to £15.

The Council have promised to help the Kickstart drugs programme, but funds are tight and they have not been yet been able to fulfil their commitment, so Christine Tooze spends a lot of time in fund-raising.

The work needs a good bank of volunteers to call on when needed. It is not a nine to five job, so they have to be committed to what they are doing. Those in the grip of drugs are very manipulative, so the volunteers have to be correspondingly tough and operate within vigorous and unbreakable rules and they must be able to communicate plainly and clearly.

The church provides homes for the addicts after detoxification so it depends heavily on volunteer homes as well as volunteer workers, and the host family gives a very positive and very necessary role model.

If cash is the limit for the residential drug centre, then finding couples both able and willing to host drug addicts must limit the alternative. The hazard that the hosts face is that they are not dealing with logic, but with people who 'click into self-destruct for no reason.' The programme has eight experienced families who are willing to take on clients who are going through the especially difficult detoxification stage.

For four years Mike and Julie, a couple with two small children, have taken people from Kickstart for the two week detox period, and none of the addicts have relapsed during that time nor did Mike and Julie ever feel in danger. Kickstart screen out anyone who might be violent, and the hosts are trained to watch for symptoms of potential risk. They do not pretend that they can be an alternative family or to look after ex-addicts for ever; just to be able to talk to them, even in the middle of the night, or provide a warm bath, and to make sure that one of them is always at home. They do have to set boundaries for behaviour and to be firm and consistent. But withdrawal is not a casual affair. It is a very tough process and emotionally draining for those who have agreed to sit it out with the addict through thick and thin.

Residential institutions such as Manna Farm or Yeldall do have the advantage of creating a spirit of mutual support, where those who know exactly how everyone else feels can help each other to pull through and make sure that mavericks do not trip them up. We once visited a residential centre in the middle of a city, where most of the clients seemed to have become addicted in prison. We asked whether there was not a strong temptation to walk down the road and get a fix. The answer was that they all kept an eye on each other. One night the warden saw a suitcase standing on the short gravel drive in front of the door. Next morning it had gone. At breakfast the mystery was solved.

> We found that Charlie was not in his room and the front door was on the latch. So we knew he'd gone out to do a job to find the money for a fix. We decided that wasn't on, so we packed all his things in his suitcase, put it outside and locked the front door behind it.

But drug addiction is still increasing and it is hard to see how the residential institutions can expand fast enough to cope. Drug addicts on the hospital list are now dying before they can get a bed. It is hard to see any model other than day care able to deal with the epidemic. Our ability to respond to the rising tide of drug addiction is probably the hardest test of the Christian church's willingness to deal with social collapse.

Prisoners and their families

It is an odd experience to meet a killer for the first time. He had been one of a gang of para-militaries, who had taken the law into their own hands. He told us,

'They'd take out one of ours, so next day we'd go out and take out one of theirs. We went on, heads down, week after week and no time to think what we were doing. Then one day I got picked up, found myself in the Maze and I kept on wondering, "There's something wrong here, it's the Shinners is meant to be here, not me." And after that, I had all the time in the world to work it out.'

Now he is out, a lot older and a lot wiser, and spends his time in giving the teenagers of North Belfast something useful to do, which would keep them away from the violence which had wasted his own youth.

In Northern Ireland, Prison Fellowship tries to help all prisoners, both para-militaries and those who call themselves ODCs, or 'ordinary decent criminals.'

Prison Fellowship was founded in post-Nixon America by Chuck Colson, senior White House legal counsel to the President, who found himself, after the Watergate scandal, pitched out of the Washington social circuit and into the steam and heat of a prison laundry. Somewhere towards the end of his time in Washington, he had experienced a genuine Christian conversion; so when he arrived in gaol, his thoughts were not of resentment, but of pity for his fellow prisoners, their bleak pasts and their even bleaker futures. America's prisons, like Britain's, were jammed to overflowing as the record prison-building programme failed to keep pace with the more rapidly growing number of prisoners – both countries' only answer to the rising tide of crime. Those in prison were out of sight and out of mind and nothing effective was being done in these dehumanising institutions to turn prisoners into ordinary decent citizens.

Prison Fellowship came to Britain in the early Eighties through the interest of Sylvia Mary Alison, whose husband, Michael, had been the Northern Ireland minister responsible for prisons. She warmed at once to Chuck Colson's vision. The Fellowship has expanded rapidly since then and it now has wise, trained and experienced visitors to 100 of Britain's 130 prisons, introduced by a card sent to every new prisoner.

The prison visitors only see those prisoners who ask for them. Some want to see them because they have no family and want someone to talk to, others because they want the Fellowship to keep in touch with their families and help with the many problems that arise through their absence. All the conversation is round a table in the visitor's wing and a good many of the visitors are men in their late fifties and early sixties, who have some experience of life.

The Fellowship is a Christian organisation and operates through and with the support of the prison chaplains. Those responsible for the prisons and having to deal with the rising tide of criminality, see more clearly than most the need for a structured, alternative life-style.

The Northern Ireland Prison Fellowship find that a major reason for the increase in crime is 'the current belief at all levels of society that there is no right and wrong.' Another is 'the high rate of unemployment and the corresponding welfare dependency (which) saps all sense of discipline. There is no need to work, no need to go to bed at night or to get up in the morning.'

They point out that, since the rate of recidivism (re-offending) is 75%

prison clearly does not work as a deterrent. Even worse, it is the university of crime and, for those not already on drugs, it is the place where they are most likely to get hooked.

When they come out, they can easily fall between the justice, probation and prison systems. One young man was released by the court on a Friday night. All the public services were closed for the weekend and he had no money and no home to go to. The easiest way to survive the weekend was to find a drug dealer and sell some drugs. Instead Prison Fellowship found sofas and food for three nights.

It is small wonder that the Director of Prison Services, Richard Tilt has thanked the Prison Fellowship's volunteers. He added, 'Many members of the public have a one-dimensional view of prison – protecting the public and improving security – without regard to rehabilitation.'

Prison Fellowship also tries to help those left outside. Life is especially hard for the wife, waiting for her man to come out. One of them wrote,

> Snubbed by my friends, friends from school days. I'm an odd number now, one instead of a couple, I'm without a man, guard your husbands well.
>
> It's me, look at me, I'm the same always, ME!
>
> To see the pain on my mother's face, her pain for my sorrow, my loneliness, my bewilderment. To see people stare, point their fingers at me.
>
> 'I'm innocent,' I want to shout, 'I haven't done anything wrong.'
>
> I'm just like you, I'm in prison too, a bigger prison, but a prison all the same. I was sentenced along with you. Ten years in prison.

So Prison Fellowship tries to offer someone to turn to, to help avoid the stress which leads to family breakdown. The Belfast branch gave help to one young mother who was left with five children and felt even more imprisoned than their father. And they also help families who have looked to the person now in prison to organise their lives and make the family decisions and don't know where to begin.

Rehabilitation is far easier if family links are kept strong, with a home and family to welcome the prisoner back. But four out of ten prisoners lose their partner during sentence. Even when they stick it out, it is not easy to pick up the pieces. A wife who has had to cope on her own becomes less dependent. Children have grown up without a father's (or mother's) guidance. And both partners change during a prison sentence.

Coming home is 'a great shock' to both the ex-prisoner and their family, so Prison Fellowship runs day release seminars to help couples work through the issues together as the sentence nears its end. And the volunteers do lunches and cream teas after release so that couples can meet others who have been through the same problems and who know the need for unconditional love to keep the marriage intact.

In the meantime the Fellowship do their best to help families to keep together. Christmas is a time when children with a parent in prison need encouragement. All their school friends are talking about their presents and they have none. So the Fellowship have set up the 'Angel Fund,' for presents to children from their absent parent. The presents cost about £7 each, which is not much, in order to encourage a sense that their absent parent still belongs to them.

Helping to make sure that partners can get to prison for visits is one of the bread and butter jobs of the Fellowship. Help is often needed, especially when home and prison are far apart. When the partner's job makes it impossible to pay a visit at the allotted time they try to provide a minivan service. They also help with letters from those who find it hard to write or to express themselves and try to be available when problems or depression become too much. As one wife said simply, 'I know the visitor's there if I want her.'

In England and Wales, a thousand families receive support and thirteen hundred children receive Christmas presents.

For every prisoner who has a family coming to visit and finally to welcome them home, there is another prisoner who has no-one to care what happens to them, who knows only the deep despair of being locked behind bars, cut off from society, rejected by family and friends, dehumanised, and robbed of dignity and purpose.

We may well feel that, with the sharp rise in crime and especially crimes of violence, they deserve all they get, that the law is too lenient and we should think more of the old who, at best fear to go out and at worst are mugged and robbed. Down at the 'Dog and Duck' they want flogging and a return of capital punishment. Christians believe that all of us, however hardened, have a conscience which tells us the difference between right and wrong, but we also believe that everyone is redeemable.

And, while all are responsible for their actions, some have less to help them keep straight. After an 'Any Questions' broadcast in a prison, I stood talking to a warder, while my wife talked to a young prisoner at the far end of the hall. The warder was keeping a steady eye on them. 'It's just as well that your wife doesn't know his form; he's one of the most dangerous we've got.' But when I talked to my wife afterwards, all she could think of was his awful family background. 'Not much wonder he got into trouble.'

Prison Fellowship is motivated by the Christian belief that there is no man or woman, whatever their offence, who is beyond God's care. Luke's account of the crucifixion of Jesus has this exchange,

> One of the criminals who hung there hurled insults at him, 'Aren't you the Christ? Save yourself and us.'

But the other criminal rebuked him, 'Don't you fear God,' he said, 'since you are under the same sentence? We are punished justly, for we are getting what our deeds deserve, but this man had done nothing wrong.' Then he turned to Jesus and said. 'Jesus, remember me when you come into your kingdom.'

Jesus answered, 'I tell you the truth, today you will be with me in paradise.'

In the famous parable of the sheep and the goats, where Jesus says that he will separate those who have true faith from those who do not by their attitude to those in need, one of his four examples of true Christian care is to visit those who are in prison.

Christ also warns his followers about their attitudes, 'Judge not that you be not judged.'

Many of those in prison come from dysfunctional families. As the Chief Inspector of Prisons has said, 'Chaotic lifestyles encourage lawbreaking and anti-social behaviour' and he believes that that is one of the main reasons for the increasing numbers being imprisoned. And the General Director of the Prison Service adds, 'We have to recognise that prisoners will return to the community, so we have to work with the prisoner and the community to improve chances of successful reintegration into society.'

Prison Fellowship is a partner in that process with the chaplains, the prison officers, the probation officers and the social services, all of whom, caught between limited resources and the steady increase in crime, are under severe pressure.

There is no doubt too that persistent high unemployment, especially among young men, is also an invitation to lawlessness. Teenagers with nothing to do and nothing to look forward to are programmed for trouble. And to this is added a sharp increase in inequality, the rich getting much richer and the poor much poorer, but seeing advertisements every day for goods they cannot hope to buy. So a sense of injustice is added to a sense of want.

Prison Fellowship aims to be as professional as those with whom it works. So the Fellowship has a careful screening process. Applicants have to have some experience of life and to be willing, above all, to listen. They must be ready to write letters, to babysit during prison visits, to organise transport for visits, to keep in touch with ex-prisoners, especially those who need a job and somewhere to live. Above all, they need patience and a real love for fellow human beings.

Prisoners know not only that the attitude of the visitors will be governed by their Christian faith, but also the advice that they give. But volunteers want to start from where the prisoner is and follow where the questions lead. They are not there to press their own faith on unwilling listeners.

All the same there has been a remarkable number of conversions to the Christian faith in British prisons in the last few years. The process seems to have started in Lewes gaol, which is a holding prison, and Christian faith has spread as prisoners who had become Christians at Lewes were sent on to prisons around the country. They may remind us of Christ's parable of the invitation to the feast, which was refused by the rich and notable, and then passed on instead to all and sundry in the highways and byways. It was they who accepted.

One of the largest providers of homes for newly released prisoners is the large Midlands charity, Adullam Homes, mentioned in the last section. The ex-prisoner with nowhere to go and no one to turn to but his comrades in crime is highly vulnerable to temptation.

Adullam's main objective is to move ex-prisoners back into the community. Their first job is to get a roof over their heads, which gives them a base until they can move on to a more permanent tenancy. Some are referred by the probation service and some get in touch directly.

The West Midlands' office of Adullam has approximately 90 places for ex-prisoners, usually in houses for two, where each has their own bedroom or self-contained accommodation.

Soon after they arrive, they are visited by one of the project workers who help them to look after their benefit claims, go through their plans for finding a job or taking courses, and suggest some constructive activities while they are waiting. The care workers are careful to respect their dignity and confidences and, as well as regular home visits, they can drop in to the office at any time during working hours.

The West Midland's care workers have to have a clear vocation for the work and all have background experience, usually working previously with offenders. Adullam also run internal training courses and support external ones, so that the staff are properly trained.

Prisoners who ask to talk to a visitor from Prison Fellowship know that it is a Christian organisation, operating with the chaplaincy, so they can be up front with their Christian position; Adullam, though also known to be a Christian organisation, feels that it is there to look after the immediate practical needs of the newly released and that its Christian input must come primarily in its care for their needs.

Projects like Adullam see the effect of prison on those who pass through their hands. They accept that prison protects the public, but the rate of reoffending shows that prison efforts at rehabilitation are ineffective; young first offenders are more likely to learn bad habits by being locked up in an exclusive criminal fraternity than to be helped to a better way of life.

2

Loose cannons

Helping the schools

The Stepping Stone Project, East Belfast

The Project is part of the East Belfast Mission on the Newtonards Road, in a district which has suffered a steep rise in unemployment as the great Harland & Wolff shipyard shrank its labour force to a fraction of its former 8,000 employees. Added to these troubles is the family break-down and homelessness, which are far more evident in the inner cities.

The Project has a job club with a 75% success rate in finding jobs or places on effective training schemes.

The part of the Project that especially caught our eyes was the home-work study centre. It was started with funds from the Prince's Trust and had initial backing from the Belfast Action Team of the Department of the Environment (Northern Ireland).

The houses in the back streets are small and overcrowded and there is nowhere for children to get quiet to concentrate, away from each other and from the TV. In the local culture homework is not the 'macho thing', so all the peer pressure is against it. Most parents are not able to help and, even if they could, single parents struggling on their own have even less time to help with homework. Other parents, who might help, are out on shift-work.

Homework needs a degree of concentration, which has to be implanted early. So the club likes to take children at six and tries to develop their motivation. It also has to find the resources that are needed for the home-work projects which are now part of the teaching and examination system.

Up to fifteen children up to age 11 come on afternoons from Monday to Thursday, where they are helped by a volunteer teacher and trainee teacher. The most noticeable effect in the schools is that their attention span increases so that they can take in far more.

Ten to fifteen children age 11-17 are looked after by two volunteer teach-ers and a trainee in the evening. Two examples of the study centre members:

Jason, (16) is now very highly motivated. He was runner-up in a 'Newsround' TV competition and, as a result was sent on a UN sponsored environment conference and, as winner of a poetry competition, has been on a trip to Chicago;

Sonia, (17) went on to help with the younger children and, because she is local, she is a good role-model for the children in the streets around.

The volunteer teachers are recruited by the organiser, Judith Rainey, herself a teacher. She pays them £12.50 a night, which is the going rate for this kind of voluntary work and she is on duty and helping every afternoon and evening. She has the ultimate responsibility for dealing with behaviour and discipline problems. She feels that the main guideline is to be positive with children and not just look at the bad things they do. She tries not to throw anyone out and was greatly encouraged by one of the worst problem boys, 'Sam', who turned out in the end to be one of the centre's best. She believes that the centre is there for children with problems as well as those without. On top of this she has to make sure that the centre complies with the safety regulations and the Child Protection Act.

Henry Bannister, a quiet, white-haired retired civil servant, looks after both the Job Club and the homework study centre and finds the £75,000 a year needed to run both of them. He says that there is always a problem, but that, somehow, they always find the money.

The Job Club is on the ground floor of a small modern building, the homework study centre on the next two floors. The building is clean and cheerful and, when the children are there, a hive of activity. It has computers for word processing which are up to the highest standards and a range of reference books which should cover all that the pupils need. It stands out as a beacon of hope, lighting the way out for those who would otherwise be trapped in aimlessness and poverty. One girl said,

'I come most nights because my pals come and we always work together. It's not really a chore when you can do it together. We do talk about other things, but we do a lot of work as well. We help each other too. Sometimes we get stuck and we get help from one of the teachers.'

Ellen Wilkinson School, Manchester

This gaunt old-fashioned school building, red-brick with high ceilings, in Manchester's inner-city district of Brunswick, has its fair share of pupils with learning difficulties. Helen Gatenby, an experienced youth worker in the district, spends a lot of her time helping the overstretched special needs teacher.

The school is ethnically mixed and, for many of the pupils, English is a second language; others have severe learning difficulties. Some come from homes where the parents cannot read and live in areas where there is long-term unemployment and within a non-literate culture: for some children, there is little incentive to learn to read. As well as these problems, the school's long-term future is uncertain with amalgamation pending, and the staff work in very demotivating circumstances – although the special needs teacher seemed bright and alert, moving from one place to another at the double!

Helen and two colleagues look after fifteen pupils between them. As she knelt at the desk of an eleven-year old, she took him gently through the reading process as if he were just beginning and it was hard to know whether, even then, he understood. Yet if she cannot get him through that reading barrier he stands little chance in life.

As we went out, we passed a girl of about eleven, standing sullenly in outdoor clothes with her school bag on her shoulder.

'Sent out, Serena?' 'Yes.' 'Something you'd done?' 'Yes.' Helen explained that sometimes things would get too much for pupils and they would create a disturbance and have to be sent out. 'They can't verbalise their problem. They have to act.'

Their only hope of escape from the dead end of inner-city unemployment is to finish well enough at school to go on to training or a job. But unless they can break the literacy barrier, there is little hope of their learning anything. To Helen and her colleagues, that is a job well worth all their time and patience.

It has one very positive knock-on effect. Helen also runs local youth clubs, and since she's been around for nine years and for a lot of young people she is a friendly and familiar figure from their school days, they are happy to give the youth clubs a try.

On the Streets

Manchester

Industry has drained away from Manchester, which used to be the throbbing centre of industrial England. First the cotton industry went, and then some of the biggest engineers' companies closed down. The motorways helped south Manchester, but they missed out the north of the city.

In one of the roughest areas of east Manchester the clinic was vandalised, burnt and abandoned, then the pub and then the shop. For safety all three buildings were demolished.

There are other parts of north Manchester which are just as violent, and where no one would think of opening a church hall for a youth club. But in a church with heavy steel doors, which serves two estates, I talked to Clare Atkins and Chris Clark, both in their twenties, who run what is called a 'street club.'

It's an area of high and chronic unemployment, so there are low expectations and high absenteeism from school. But Chris lives on one of the estates, so he is seen as one of them and when he and Clare and one or two other volunteers watch the lads kicking a football around on the concrete pitch by the primary school, its not too hard to make friends.

Clare helps with RE teaching in the school and Chris, who is a computer buff, says that he 'hangs round the IT room' to help them with internet access.

The few boys who do go to the church are a beginning and when Chris and Clare suggest some activities outside the estates, they bring along their friends to make up a party. The girls are not interested in the boys' activities, so in practice the club is for boys.

The choice of activity is decided by the boys. They go swimming, go-carting, dry-skiing and nine-pin bowling. The most popular is a wide game on the hills outside Oldham, called 'into the light,' where the aim is to get back into base without being seen by the defenders' two bright lights. They also enjoy Quasar, a sophisticated version of the same game, with electronic packs to register the hit of a light beam from a laser gun. If the team, which includes two volunteers, show respect to the lads, they usually show respect in return. Only once has someone had to be sent home. On the way home there is a ritual call for fish and chips and a five minute talk. In the summer they go camping above Morcambe Sands and pay visits to Blackpool.

Like those who are really competent in their work, Chris and Clare make it seem easy. But the majority of pupils in the local school have been excluded from some other school and it has one of the highest truancy rates in the country. The school tries to get its pupils places in technical college at 15 so that they can learn a trade; but it is a hard battle to win through against hopelessness and inertia with so many in the second or third generation of school dropouts.

They both find that the teenagers get very short-tempered with each other. The girls take the lads apart verbally and the lads, who can't compete verbally, become very destructive physically and throw the furniture around.

Chris and Clare would not stand out in a crowd and maybe it is that laid-back look which helps them to get alongside the teenagers. And they do have the great advantage over the club leader who has to protect the church hall from those who see it as a challenge to their powers of destruction. Their teenagers need the minibus to get to the game and back again afterwards. All the same, the leaders need to know where the limit of tolerance should be and how to stay in control when it is reached. But of all the gifts, the greatest of all, to quote the Apostle Paul, is love, and it must be that quality, rare on a rough estate of dysfunctional families, which shines through and commands respect.

Glasgow

Glasgow has been as hard hit as any British city by the loss of key industries and the jobs they gave. In inner city Glasgow, as elsewhere, the need to come to the homeless where they are and on their own terms is self-evident: many of them are only teenagers. The Glasgow City Mission decided that it had to do something for those who were roofless, and found funding for a Vauxhall Frontera. This Night Patrol vehicle adopted fairly regular parking places which meant that the teenager homeless met the mission staff on their own ground, and because they also felt respected, were happy to stop and talk.

Many of the teenagers living on the street are very isolated and vulnerable. A large number have suffered abuse and therefore find it hard to build good relationships, but some do form limited friendships. Glasgow City Mission staff and volunteers try to build trust through regular caring contact. To help them to build stronger relationships, staff take some of them out to activities, such as five-a-side football, badminton, hillwalking and to camps in the summer.

One in three children in Glasgow live in poverty and most of these live in 'troubled or broken homes, which makes it very difficult for them to build a secure lifestyle for themselves.' A study of young people in the Castlemilk area, a large area of urban deprivation, shows that schoolchildren of seven years old have similar expectations to those in a nearby affluent area, but by the time they are teenagers these expectations have gone. They also have the same abilities as the other children, but much lower expectations, and so they don't bother going to school. In this way their lack of self-esteem is self-fulfilling. Generation after generation of unemployment and poverty brings with it a lack of hope and 'a deepening negativity'.

Teenage girls who become homeless or addicted to drugs can end up in prostitution. A study done by Glasgow University identified about 250 girls in Glasgow's red light district. Many of these women came to the Mission's Night Patrol for soup and sandwiches and, knowing that the homeless men had a mission shelter, they wanted their own, somewhere they could go for food and care and, for those who had suffered violence from their clients, for refuge.

So the Mission took over a redundant pub as an evening refuge, and up to eighty girls would drop in and out of an evening. Eventually the two pubs and the shop which were all being used for the homeless were replaced by a new multi-purpose building, known as the Shieling, one part of which is for the street girls, 80% of whom are on heroin or other drugs. They are in a 'catch 22': only the drugs make prostitution bearable, but they needed the money from prostitution to buy the drugs.

The hope of the Mission is, of course, that the girls will come off the streets. They use specialists from other agencies for drug rehabilitation and they have a lunch club, so that the girls can come in in the daytime with their families and enable the Mission staff to get to know both them and their children. It is easier to reach them in Glasgow than in other cities because there is less organised pimping than elsewhere. This makes the girls more vulnerable to violence from clients, but it is easier for them to come off the streets. There is a problem, however, for those girls with drug-addicted partners, who depend on their income from prostitution to fund the habit.

Some girls in rehabilitation have to go to court for debt default and the Mission goes with them, giving letters to the court about the efforts which they were making and arguing that prison would be a real setback. The Mission sometimes finds the money to pay small fines and helps them to find employment and housing. Quite a number have come off the streets and are married with a home. Some have also been reunited with their children.

The Mission has also developed a property on the outskirts of Glasgow as a 'Crisis Support Centre' for women, a place of security, safety and peace, in which their lives can begin to be healed.

The Mission is fully supported by several local churches. Some of these churches are good at giving a warm welcome to those who, however strange their personal history, have become firm Christians through the mission.

Mission staff and volunteers do not press their Christian faith on those who come for help, but they hope that it is shown in the way that they express Christian compassion and love for the whole person. A growing number of those they help have become Christians.

It is very hard for the Mission to get any precise measure of the outcome of all their efforts, but the people they try to help are, one way or another, certainly better off than they were before. The most dramatic changes appear in the lives of those who do become Christians. Graeme Clark, the Director, says, 'Part of caring holistically means caring for both the practical and the spiritual needs of the individual. Secular agencies cannot talk of holistic care if they are not helping people spiritually. They can disagree with Christians, but they cannot leave out a part of human nature.'

Graeme Clark is the inspiration behind the present form of the Glasgow City Mission and it is he who has made the City feel that it is their own mission and that they must support it.

Founded in the year 1826, eleven years after the Battle of Waterloo, and the first city mission in the world, it had become, ten years ago, a collection of mission halls, most duplicating the services of the local churches. It was also £30,000 a year in the red. Graeme Clark, who was a Baptist minister in Kirkaldy, was asked by the Trustees to do a report.

He had been running an unemployment resource centre with training courses and had wide experience of community work. They accepted his report and asked him to take over the Mission and implement it.

He closed most of the mission halls and started the present work of direct care for the needy. As the Mission was no longer running its own churches and was doing much-needed new work it started to gain more support from the Glasgow churches. He made the change in the basis of the work widely known, and started to advertise in *The Herald*, a Scottish broadsheet. He has also built up a donor base, and the current income is £500,000 a year. The advertisements in the Herald work out at only 10% of the annual increase in income. He says, 'Christian people like professionalism. Their view is that Christian work should be better than any other and, as a result, the work and the money to fund it seem to increase together.'

The Shieling multicare centre, with a medical block and separate sections for men and women, cost £178,000. Glasgow City Council, the Development Agency and the Health Service each gave £30,000 and the Mission raised the remainder within two months.

The Mission has a professional partnership with other agencies, such as the Greater Glasgow Health Board, and it organises a GP service, nursing, dental care, mental health care, pediatrics and physiotherapy for needy people. Its own staff is twenty plus and they are supported by eighty volunteers.

Some other City Missions might usefully look at this pattern. They all, of course, have their specialities; but the overwhelming needs are those with which the Glasgow City Mission is dealing; so it could be that other City Missions could find the same financial, church and volunteer support. Bearing the city's name is a great help in raising support, as Coventry and Southampton have found in organising the City Networks which we describe in Chapter Six.

Youth Projects

Romsey Mill, Cambridge

While the 1980s brought depression in industrial Britain, Cambridge was a growth area, sprouting high-tech companies small and large, all encouraged by the unique partnership between the University and business. Since then, the city has never looked back. But even Cambridge has its poorer end, the small Victorian terrace houses leading off the Mill Road on the east side of the railway bridge, described as 'an area of low academic achievement.'

Half a mile beyond the railway bridge and in the heart of the district is Romsey Mill, an old Methodist church, turned into a youth club twenty years ago. The Mill, as it's known locally, has a long-standing relationship with the nearby secondary school and organises informal school groups for outside activities. The staff of the Mill form these 'Small Groups' into football teams or for other sports or outings and, as the groups get to know the Mill, they ask friends to come with them, giving very strong roots for the Mill in the local community.

The Mill also caters for those left far behind by the city's high-tech society, teenagers who find it difficult to relate to an older generation, are not part of the school's Small Groups and also find it hard just to walk into a youth club where no one knows them. So the workers at the Mill don't sit around waiting for the teenagers to come. They go out to parks and schools, where they meet those they already know, and, through them, are able to invite others in to the Mill's programme. They don't press an invitation at the first meeting, but come back to talk again and take time with them. Andrew Lloyd got to know Kerry, John and Carl among others and spent time with them, simply building up mutual trust and respect. When they all had confidence in him, they came into the Mill one night a week to use the internet and computers and to play indoor football. But it was soon clear that it was not just the activities which attracted them, but the respect which Andrew and his fellow-worker, Martin gave them. They had never thought much of themselves, and now they began to feel some self-worth.

At school they were completing their GCSEs and the encouragement which they had at the Mill, though free of any pressure, kept them at it, and when they left school they all managed to find jobs. It didn't stop there. They had discovered their real potential at the Mill and wanted to make their own contribution, so they decided to start up a Romsey Mill football team.

Andrew also got to know Bill who came to the Mill, but was thrown out of school at fifteen. He found a job in a garage, but he got into trouble with the police, lost his job and came back to Andrew for help. Andrew went with him to the three court hearings and afterwards sat with him in a café talking over the issues and helping him, as a friend, to face up to the consequences of what he had done and to say he was sorry and that he would sort out his life. Without Andrew's friendly help, he would almost certainly not have made and meant those commitments. Then he found another job, which he has been able to hold.

Though there are a lot of seasonal and temporary jobs in Cambridge, many of the young people find it much harder to find a permanent job with long-term prospects. To help them, the Mill have been asked by the City Council to set up a Job Club for those over sixteen and, since Andrew has a good relationship with this group, he has now started the Job Club, helping them with CVs, letter writing, and application forms. Sue Bailey from Cambridge Jobsearch is the Club tutor.

Romsey Mill also has a young parent's support project, for single mothers, run by Liz Diamond.

Life for single mothers is tough, facing the normal stresses and strains of parenting alone and also making her feel isolated from mothers with husbands, who know nothing of her troubles. They usually have tensions in their relations with their own families and many live on the poverty line. Since they are so much younger than all the other mothers they find it very hard to integrate with the normal network of ante and post-natal provision and parent support groups. Liz Diamond tries to give them some of the support they need and to help them to help each other and to take a positive attitude to bringing up their children.

They all have troubled histories. Melanie's troubles started when she began to be bullied at school by girls who had been her closest friends. She spent less and less time at school. Then she discovered that she was pregnant, but hid it from everyone until, one day, she was out shopping and fainted, because she had gone into labour. The new baby in the home was a great shock to her family and she went to other relatives. Then she heard about the group at Romsey Mill, and Liz was able to help re-establish relations with her family and the group have rallied round and helped her cope.

Sarah was eighteen when she found that she was pregnant and she and her partner looked forward to parenthood. But the scan showed that she was expecting twins and her partner disappeared. She had to go to hospital alone in a taxi and her partner could not cope with the fact that he was the father of two babies. She never saw him again. She found the group at the Mill a great support and having, after a year, found a flat of her own, she seems to Liz to be through the worst.

Jane was working for her 'A'-levels when she found that she was four months pregnant. She moved in with her partner and started her first year at college, but after two weeks, he left her for someone else. She moved back to her parents, but, when the baby arrived, the pressure with other children already in the family became too great. She had to move out to a flat with no central heating and a long way from buses and shops and felt very isolated. The health visitor sent her to the Mill and, meeting regularly with others of her own age who were facing the same problems made all the difference.

These young parents feel that they are being judged by older and more 'sorted' parents and feel defensive against the usually unspoken, but very clear belief that they are stupid for getting pregnant so young. Their different life-styles also create a barrier. So, as well as having the groups in the Mill, the staff also visit them in their homes for one to one chats, and arrange lessons for them in parenting skills.

The Under Fives Programme is run by Rachel Matthews, a comfortable mother of three who has also been a nursery school teacher. They have what they call Messy Mornings, sixty plus children 'painting everything in sight'. There are also about forty in a class for older children and the staff say that the mothers get as much out of each other's company as the children.

The centre is open to people to drop in without appointment and it has an alcohol free bar open five nights a week. This, with the computers and the sports hall helps to make it a social centre for the young people in the district and keeps them off the streets.

Romsey Mill was founded by three local churches and all the board members are Christians, as are most of the paid staff. The Mill draws on the churches for volunteer workers and has a Christian statement of faith and an annual service of thanks. But it sees itself as a public service in the city, not as a church or even a para-church organisation and is careful not to proselytise. It will have outside speakers from time to time, some of whom are Christians and some not.

The staff believe that it is the care for those who come to the Mill which should be the best evidence of their Christian faith. They pray together for those whom they are trying to help and tell the children the stories of Christmas and Easter and other bible stories. If older ones ask them about their faith, they feel free to respond, but never to bring any pressure.

But, though the Mill itself is not seen as overtly religious, it does not hide its Christianity and, amongst many activities, takes young people to Christian summer camps. Last summer, for instance, nine of them, aged between ten and thirteen, went with volunteer staff to an activity centre near Sevenoaks where they joined thirty others in swimming, assault courses, go-karting, abseiling and archery, and on outings.

Those who run the Mill feel that they have learnt the hard way how to establish relations with teenagers in today's volatile society. So, when asked, they were happy to pass on its experience to ordinands at one of the University's Anglican theological colleges, Ridley Hall, in a new course combining theological study with professional youth work.

Cambridge churches support Romsey Mill financially and by helping them to find staff. The Chairman and three of the staff, for instance, are members of Eden Chapel and one of these staff is responsible for finding the vital voluntary workers. And the funding needed is not small. The estimated total for 1998 is £160,000, but donations local and national are expected to cover it. The professionalism of the staff and their good management has earned respect not only from users and the local community, but in hard cash from the donors.

There are bigger, older and more famous youth clubs than Romsey Mill; but it is perhaps a better role model for those churches who feel that they could develop an old club or start up a new one in an area which has not reached disaster level but still has more than its fair share of poverty and social need.

There is no obvious specification for the kind of person who should run a youth club. My wife and I were once trustees of a youth club in Clapham, supported by Westminster Chapel. The woman who ran it came from an old county family and her last full-time job had been as a programme researcher for the BBC. But she turned out to be perfect for the job. She had a booming 'county' voice, which seemed to command instant respect among the warring 'mods' and 'rockers' who demanded entry. She kept them apart by making them come on separate nights and, as they arrived at the door, insisted that they each surrender his knife to her, and she carefully returned his knife to each as they left.

Chris Rose at the Mill is quite different. But his height certainly commands respect and his laid-back, unfussy manner seems just right to give confidence to the young. But behind the casual manner is a combination of wisdom, patience and persistence, which has done the Mill great service.

The M 13 Youth Project, Manchester

Urban Action Manchester, a part of the national movement 'Youth for Christ' has developed three projects in inner city areas of Manchester, each of which run along the same principles and values. One of these is the M13 Youth Project which, in partnership with local churches, works in schools, on the streets and in clubs with young people at risk of being marginalised by society.

The work is led by Helen Gatenby, the youth worker mentioned above, and the project currently has two other workers as well. The main objective is to establish relationships with young people at risk, listen to them and work together with them to create youth activities. Through these relationships and activities workers support and enable young people to be creative, engage with issues and improve the quality of their lives and their communities.

Another feature of the work is its close partnership with local churches, with the aim of training up youth workers from the local area. But example is worth far more than theory. So the project staff work alongside volunteers from local churches, training 'on-the-job' and enabling work to be established and owned by local churches. The project has done this with three churches, facilitating work that meets the needs of the young people and that is appropriate to the resources available locally.

Helen has lived in the district for nine years and, with her work in the principle school, is a well-known figure to many young people locally. Helen and her team work in schools three days a week, supporting pupils who are struggling to succeed or even stay within the education system. The government's emphasis on raising educational standards means that schools can be under pressure to exclude pupils who may jeopardise their hard-won place in a league table. And at the moment government still seems reluctant to tackle the clear correlation between poverty and under-achievement, presumably because to do so would require more funding and higher taxes – something the majority of the electorate are not happy to vote for. The work of the M13 project is important in helping to redress the basic injustice which means that some young people are not given the same opportunities and resources as others.

On Mondays, they help with the small Christian group in the school. On Tuesdays they run a girls group and a lads group – they do the same for older teenagers on a Thursday, when they invite the groups to meet in their homes or a church building. On Wednesdays they spend time with a group of young black teenage men on some kind of organised activity, outdoors like go-karting or games in a church hall. They also take groups away on residentials, where young people get a chance to try outdoor pursuits and activities, to which they don't have access in a city centre. They are in the process of establishing a new piece of work, meeting kids who are not attached to any sort of youth group in their own setting, usually on the streets.

Through activities and relationships, workers see many young people developing and making positive changes. But they also face difficult moral decisions as youth workers and Christians when working with young people engaged in criminal activity, such as stealing cars or doing drugs. It is by no means an easy decision for workers to sort out where their loyalties lie, especially as judging a young person too quickly, will damage and sometimes ruin a promising relationship. Workers have found that inappropriate behaviour can more easily be addressed and changed within a committed relationship between the worker and the young person. When a young person knows that the worker cares for them and is concerned for their best interests, they can trust that the challenge to their behaviour is not simply the result of judgmentalism and rejection.

Some members of these youth groups face all kinds of problems and the small team of three and local church volunteers deal with them as they are able. One girl was overwhelmed by the problems in her family. Her parents divorced when she was eleven and she felt rejected by her dad. She suffered a number of close family and neighbour bereavements, leaving her grieving, depressed and stressed. And, with all these pressures, she struggled in school, became aggressive and got into street fighting as a way of dealing with her anger. It took a lot of time and patience to bring some measure of healing.

In a culture of dysfunctional relationships, and especially their implications within families, few people know how to resolve conflict, to say sorry or to accept an apology. Teenagers find many adults hostile and do not know how to relate to them. But the team have found that these teenagers can and do relate to friendly adults. The only way in is to build individual relationships, seeing them in school and on the streets out of school and then helping them to develop the whole person.

Helen and her small Urban Mission team have taken the most difficult first step for inner city youth work and aim to offer training so that others can follow where they have started. Already the Evangelical Coalition have asked them to run a training workshop on Urban mission. Helen is as passionate about helping the teenagers on the streets make the best of their lives as she is about helping the struggling pupils at school make the big breakthrough. If anyone can spark enthusiasm, she can!

Teenage pregnancy

Whatever way we look at it, abortion is a very emotive issue. On the one hand it is at the heart of the movement for women's rights. On the other, it is seen as killing a child, which a mother's instinct tells her to protect.

Many women are torn apart by the conflict of emotions they feel when faced with the difficulties of lone parenthood and yet sense an instinctive desire to care for their baby. Teenagers, being less experienced in life, can feel especially overwhelmed at the enormity of the decisions facing them.

Five years ago we went to the Firgrove Centre in Southampton, which offered free pregnancy tests and soon began to have a steady stream of women who could not afford to buy a pregnancy test from the chemist. It was in a converted shop and decorated in pretty and restful colours, with easy chairs and a quiet, gentle lady in charge, to whom it was easy for anyone to pour out their troubles.

Shortly afterwards another centre was started in nearby Basingstoke and there is now a network of over 100 centres in Britain, under the name of Care for Life.

The Firgrove Centre is backed by a number of churches in Southampton, who want to offer help and compassion to women facing an unplanned pregnancy. Rather than moralising, the counsellors offer accurate information about the three options open to pregnant women: continuing with the pregnancy, adoption and abortion. All three options are sensitively explored with regard to how they might affect the woman. The centre provides a safe place where they can talk and be listened to.

The Southampton Centre sees about 140 women a month, some of whom have come for the free test and others referred by their GPs. They explain the arrangements for adoption, explore the help needed for keeping the baby and how it might be found. They also talk about post-abortion stress, which affects about a significant proportion of women who have an abortion, and causes 10% to need psychiatric help.

They also offer post-abortion counselling to women who are left with a sense of loss, grief and guilt. A great many of these have had an abortion because of pressure from their partner, parents or friends. Many are unprepared for the emotions they feel, having chosen what they felt was the best option under difficult circumstances. This is why the Centre tries to help those who still need to come to a decision to make their own choice, based on full information and on their own feelings.

A woman's instinct may be to keep the baby, but she may also feel trapped by the problems and pressures. Some young women come from broken homes, where they have experienced a lack of love and affection, and hoped to find it in a sexual relationship. Peer pressure also makes teenage sex a 'rite of passage' to being an adult and it is, of course, heavily promoted by magazines, films, TV and videos, not to mention their boy-friends. A few girls are as young as 13, but the norm is 14 or 15.

Rachel was just 17 when she came to the Centre with her mother. She and her boyfriend had split up and her parents were in the middle of a divorce. She was very shocked by the result of the test. She didn't want an abortion, but, with her life in turmoil, she didn't want to add to her mother's problems and didn't see what else she could do. The counsellor talked to both of them and then to her mother on her own and they left without making a decision.

Two years later the counsellor met Rachel's mother, who told her that Rachel had had the baby and she had been able to help her while she carried on at school. She had got excellent grades in the 'A'-levels and was looking for a university where she could find child care.

The Southampton Centre run an educational programme called 'Choices' in local secondary schools, and it is now in strong demand.

It is aimed at 14 to 16 year-olds and through interactive methods of teaching and learning raises the issues surrounding relationships. They aim to encourage people to have relationships that respect both their own personality and that of their friends. They ask them to think about what they believe to be important in relationships and also to understand the emotional and physical effects of sexual activity in relationships. They encourage discussion of the issues in 'an non-judgmental setting' and hope that, instead of just giving in to peer pressure, this will help teenagers to make up their own minds.

They also look at the development of the unborn baby and encourage students to discuss their attitude to abortion. And they look at the nature and transmission of the HIV virus, as well as other common sexually transmitted diseases, so that they are all aware of the risks.

They began by visiting two schools and that has now risen to eight, with a hundred and fifty talks a year.

Another group which tries to help teenage girls is the Luton Churches Education Trust, which sends counsellors to schools which ask for them.

Jo White, one of the counsellors who works for the Trust, says that ideally good relationships should be role modelled and taught in the family. But given the very high number of divorces, the family cannot be the role model for a great many girls.

She says, 'Teachers and other professionals in schools seem to be able to list off the top of their heads the young people they know who will be most at risk of pregnancy.' These are the disaffected pupils, who are less likely to listen to anything taught them in school. They are all the children listed as most at risk; children of teenage mothers, the homeless, young offenders, the very poor, persistent truants and those from broken families. These are the ones who suffer from lack of self-esteem and lack of affection and care.

Many of these children are not able to link an action with its consequences, a problem which criminologists find in their work with very violent offenders. So, though education is a help to those who listen and an especial help to those whose families simply will not discuss sex, it is clear that education alone is not enough, it is necessary to establish relationships, which is what the Churches Education Trust tries to do. Jo White says,

> The simplistic answer would be to accept that teenagers are likely to be sexually active, so they should just be plied with free contraception. But we have to look at the reasons why they want to get involved early in sexual relationships. Long-term change in attitudes is largely dependent on the role models of slightly older teenagers and adults. We as adults are often inconsistent in our attitudes, saying, "Don't do this," and doing it ourselves.

'Young people need to know why they shouldn't have sex so early. There is need for high quality teaching from credible and consistent adults on sex and relationships. It must tackle the core issues that seem to drive teenagers into the relationships – often abusive and destructive – which lead to pregnancy. Issues such as self-worth, self-esteem, values and consequences need to be put in an engaging manner and there needs to be some sort of strategy to reach and teach those excluded from school.'

Jo meets with other girls she has got to know through the schools work, girls who are from stable family backgrounds, who have been 'well brought up,' but 'think they know enough to be sexually active without becoming pregnant. It is sheer risk-taking. At the time they don't care about the consequences and just seize the day. Some arrogantly assume that they will not be affected.'

'Younger teenage girls who become pregnant nearly always have older boyfriends and if they become pregnant it makes them extremely distrustful, either because they feel that they should have been warned or because their boyfriend told them that they would not become pregnant. They are also too young to deal with the depression that results from the miscarriages that often happen to teenagers.'

Girls like this need support, which is what Jo tries to give them. Like the staff in Firgrove, she takes them through the options and, because she does not press a particular view, she retains the trust of teachers, who refer girls to her. Some, because they know her, come to her directly. And the schools' welfare officers are likely to take her advice on how best to support a girl.

Those of us who remember a time when the family was not in crisis know the protection which used to be there, the much loved older brothers with whom a younger sister would contrast the boyfriends who wanted to take advantage of her vulnerability. There was the affection within the family circle which would make her hesitate to offend or embarrass father or mother, the warm encouragement from them which would make her feel her own self-worth. That voluntary safe haven of the teenage years has been destroyed by the break-up of the family.

The family was not perfect and the abuse of parental power and influence in keeping true hearts apart was the theme of thousands of romantic novels, but institutions should be judged by their proper use and not by their exceptional abuse, and the disappearance of this circle of trust and affection has spelt tragedy for millions of lives.

Teenage mothers

Drumchapel Emmaus Family Project, Glasgow

The Drumchapel estate stands on a windy hill above the Clyde west of Glasgow. North-west and north-east are golf courses and beyond them are richer suburbs of Glasgow. But when the Drumchapel estate was built, it looked to Clydeside and the shipyards for work. The shipyards, which led the world and launched the great transatlantic Cunarders and which helped to build the Royal Navy, have now vanished. It was not entirely the fault of the workers. Management had become complacent and slack, so the international shipping companies went to Japan and then Korea, whose shipbuilders had made huge investments in new yards and whose prices were far lower.

Glasgow City put funds into the Drumchapel Project, which we visited in 1994, meeting the residents committee, who had a big say on the refurbishment of the housing and the new social projects. Two years later, when the Drumchapel Project ran out of money, Linda Dunnett, wife of a Church of Scotland minister, was working for 'The Dove,' a project for teenage mums. She felt that it should be saved if at all possible and the West Glasgow New Church, a Brethren Assembly, set up a Trust, made some of their elders trustees gave initial funding and brought in partner Evangelical churches.

The churches now backing the project found volunteers and the local Women's Guild of the Church of Scotland backed them up. The churches give the project a slot in the Sunday service or in a main mid-week meeting so that they can keep in touch and they continue to produce volunteers and gifts in kind.

Unlike so many other city estates, there is a strong community feeling in Drumchapel. The social structure is still quite strong and so is the wider family, where there is still a network of grandparents and cousins who are willing to support a single mother. But all the other problems are there, poverty, debt and lifestyle. There is violence too. Some are in trouble with the law. Tempers are short and they get into fights with each other. Some are involved in minor frauds.

Abortion is unacceptable to three-quarters of the girls.

A lot of fathers walk out during the pregnancy. Some go because the teenage mother suddenly has a job and the boy, hanging around in a small flat, becomes just another mouth to feed and their friends advise, 'get rid of the fella.' The mother usually has tenancy of the flat and they are not married, so he has no legal status. In one way or another, the fathers disappear.

> Those who are on hard drugs develop a vacant look as if you're not there. Those who have been on cannabis begin to lose their memory and say, 'I know I can't remember because of the hash.' There is an increasing drugs problem and heroin has come in in the last two years.

The project sends those who want to come off drugs on to other local youth movements who deal with the problem.

Some children are sent into care and come back with new clothes and new trainers, which they wouldn't have got otherwise, and they begin to look at a time in care as a right or a way to get a new pair of trousers. So there is a real danger that care creates a dependency culture. Despite new clothes, they all have a problem of low self-esteem and lack confidence in themselves.

The Trust has twelve volunteers including Linda Dunnett. Two are teachers, two run the crèche, two sit and chat with the young mums, two are 'befrienders,' who take them for outings. One man plays snooker with the dads, two look after the younger girls and there is one other part-time paid staff member. When furniture needs to be moved, she commandeers her husband and two sons to help them.

The children find it hard to concentrate on homework in their cramped homes so two teachers run an after-school club twice a week to help them.

The Trust runs a 'lifeskills' class once a week in a local church for just under twenty girls, with talks about health, hygiene, safety, money, justice and bringing up children. The social services send along experts on some of these subjects. As well the talks, they make pictures, cards and jewellery, the church lays on coffee and soup and there is a crèche for their children.

Most of the girls want, above all, someone to talk to. There is a teenage group for girls of thirteen to seventeen two nights a week. They began one for older girls, but most of them prefer to drop in to the centre for one to one talks or, especially if they have children, to have Linda or another volunteer go to talk to them at home.

Linda Dunnett has the heaviest work-load, which she reckons at forty eight hours a week, because she has a good rapport with the older girls, often baking with them while talking. They are all extremely frank and open with her and hold very little back.

The Scottish Head Office of Lloyds Bank Trustee Savings Bank helped with a large initial donation and, despite their strong connection with the local churches, most of their income so far has come through Trusts. The trustees have Linda's husband as an advisor, as well as a lady who can give good advice about which charitable trusts to ask for help.

Orchard Family Centre, Peckham

The superficial contrast with the closely knit community of Drumchapel could not be greater. 75% are from Black and other minority groups and half of the families will move within a year.

The other contrast is that many of the parents in Peckham, especially the single parents, are often isolated and on low incomes, and sometimes also lack a support network of family and friends.

Nita Rogers, who is the manager of The Orchard Family Centre in Peckham, says that the Centre 'is committed to enabling, supporting and empowering families under pressure. It is committed to helping people 'to have a hope and a future'.

The Centre in Peckham is bigger than the one in Drumchapel, with a wider range of activities and more paid workers. Its current services include the Pre-school, parenting courses (including teen parenting), a Toy Book Video Library, and an Advice and Information Service. The Centre aims to be 'responsive to the needs of the family, helping them to find innovative ways through life's challenges, professional in the planning, delivery and evaluation of its services, preventative by identifying and anticipating areas of pressure and providing services that address those areas.'

The area has a short supply of affordable childcare provision, so the Centre provides low-cost pre-school education and care. The Centre is welcoming, homely and good fun, and parents know that the children will enjoy themselves and are in good hands so that they don't have to worry about what they are up to. When the children go to school, they will hopefully be able to face its challenges with more confidence than they might otherwise have had.

A new initiative of the Centre has been the Teen pre-parenting course, which addresses some of the vital issues of underage teen pregnancies and the demands of being a teenage parent. The sessions include subjects such as Taking Charge of Your Life, Choices and Responsibilities, The Needs of the Child, Demands of Teen Parenthood, and Parenting Skills. Southwark has the highest rate of underage teen pregnancies in Europe. The Centre is developing a handbook to support schools in addressing the issue of teenage pregnancy. The following comments were made by two pupils who attended the course:

> I have learnt how difficult it would be to be a parent. I have learnt how important it is to give children attention when they are being good and praise them so they can keep doing good things . . . to have patience with them and teach them to have respect for others.
>
> I have learnt a lot about how to respect myself, to rethink my future as a parent and the sort of parent I want to be . . . how to cope with my children and how to bring them up.

The Centre is part of the Ichthus Peckham and Dulwich Church. All its eight staff work part time and many of the Centre's initiatives are facilitated by volunteer teams from church who are well-trained, committed and professional with a vision for social action.

The church provided £10,000 to launch the Centre and provide an ongoing £2,000 a year and about £3,500 comes in individual covenants. In 1998 there were grants from BBC Children in Need, four other trusts and UK Action, all of which covered specific activities. There is one part-time fund-raiser and money comes from fund-raising events, and donations from churches, companies and individuals as well as the trusts.

Adullam Homes, Leicester refuge

There comes a time in a dysfunctional family when its weakest members feel that they can endure no more. Just outside Leicester city centre is a secure hostel, staffed day and night by paid workers, where women can go with their small children when the violence is unendurable. We asked Kathryn Stacey, who is in charge of the hostel and the two other women's hostels nearby, what it was that triggered their flight. She said that it was often alcohol or drugs. All kinds of conflicts may have led up to that point, but that was what usually brought on the violence.

Most of the women who came were between sixteen and twenty-five and had small children. Some of them knew the hostel, some were sent by the social services, some by the probation service. If their partners come after them, they are turned away and if they threaten violence, the staff send for the police. There is a large Asian population in Leicester, and there are also refuges for Asian women escaping from domestic violence. The hostel, which is part of Adullam Homes, has twelve self-contained flats, where the women cook for themselves, but there is a communal sitting room where they all encourage each other and create a great feeling of solidarity.

There is a staff of three project workers at this hostel, which is open all twenty-four hours. These staff help the women to get through all the paperwork needed for social security and housing benefit, change the children's school and doctor if that is necessary, help them find college courses or training if needed and generally give them support through the crisis. The women stay for an average of six months, though the younger ones may need longer and extra help to organise their lives and to develop life skills and parenting skills.

The staff are especially concerned for the children, some of whom have behavioural difficulties, and see that they get to nursery school. They would very much like to add a crèche when funds are available.

The hostel is owned by Adullam's housing association and the income comes from housing benefit and the City Council. The churches help with a welfare fund, which is used for outings and Christmas presents.

Kathryn Stacey said that there was no explicit Christian teaching. The management committee always open with prayer and the women are often there to discuss some issue, so it is clear that it is a Christian organisation. And staff answer questions about their own Christian faith, but they believe that their main responsibility is to show Christian care and not to press their own views.

Living with AIDS

However tough it may be to try to help drug addicts, or the tough teenagers in the big estates, there are always the prospects of a life turned round, of people who have found their strengths and can go on to make their own way and their own contribution to family and community. But those helping the housebound sufferers of AIDS are always living in the shadow of death and they need a very special brand of resilience and compassion.

Debbie Werner has been a volunteer with ACET (AIDS Care and Education Trust) for three years and usually looks after a couple of clients at a time. First she has to build up their trust and confidence. They need to know that they are not being discussed behind their backs. Then she has to strike a balance between professionalism and the friendship that helps to build up their much-needed emotional support. She says that it can be heart-rending to see their health deteriorate and that is what makes the work such a challenge.

The actual physical work is to do for the client what they can no longer do for themselves: keeping the home tidy and clean, housekeeping, cooking and shopping. She tries to care for them as she would want someone to care for her, and to be punctual and courteous. The clients know that ACET is a Christian organisation, so their expectations are high. As they get to know her, they will sometimes ask about her faith and beliefs, which she is free to discuss, but only if she is asked.

Marjorie Parrot, another volunteer, says that she greatly admires the resilience of her clients in coping with 'difficult and constraining circumstances' and, though the work is strictly professional, it doesn't stop her caring or worrying about them and the death of a client, when it comes, hits hard, however well prepared she may be.

She says that to be a volunteer needs flexibility, a sense of humour, the willingness to get one's hands dirty and to serve as one equal to another. Especially for those who have no one else to see them or care for them, the regular visits give them someone they can always trust.

The service provided by ACET home care is both personal and practical and volunteers do whatever is needed, including transport to and from the hospital, help with bathing and showering, or simply providing company. Sometimes help is needed with taking children to school and babysitting.

Volunteers in this harrowing work need support themselves. They are backed by local support groups and are told to ring the organiser's office whenever they feel the need. Sometimes it is the overworked organisers themselves who need help. On our first visit to one local project there were two organisers. On our second there was only one, who was badly overstretched, and on our third, the stress had become too great and she too had had to give up.

It is a job with a very high degree of dependency. This last organiser told us, 'Their partners have gone and so have their friends and their family don't want to know them. They are often entirely on their own. We are the only people they see on a regular basis.' Death is the great unmentionable today and people don't know what to say to those who are gripped in its inexorable advance. Even in the churches, people would sooner volunteer for and fund a work with a positive outcome. Added to that is the need to sift out from the volunteers the kind of people who could not meet the demands of this traumatic job.

Yet, despite the occasional failures, the work goes on. The biggest local organisation of ACET is in London. Half their clients are African women and the other half are gay men, with a few drug users and sufferers from heterosexual infections in addition. Almost all are referred by the local authority.

For the Africans there are cultural barriers which prevent sufferers from AIDS from talking with their family about their condition. Ian Marden, co-ordinator of volunteers at ACET in London, says that 'even in the gay community the disease is a 'no-no' and those who admit infection risk losing friendship and support.' He says that volunteers need to be people who can deal with the specific issues which AIDS raises; death, rejection, and homosexuality, and to be able to serve the individual sufferer. Recruitment is by word of mouth or through ACET's general publicity. They interview, train, and make on-the-job assessment.

Some clients want only the minimum amount of contact with the carer, others are so open that they will want to spend time with carers after their duties have finished. The trust built up between carer and client promotes trust in ACET as an organisation. One client said, 'The contact and friendliness of your staff is beyond reproach; they give the feeling that there is no trouble doing anything I ask.'

ACET, which was started in 1988, also has offices in Brighton, Chichester, Northampton, South Wales, Clydeside and Tayside, as well as an increasing number of overseas operations in as many as five continents. It provides altogether for about four hundred people living at home. Its funding is half-statutory, from contracts with twenty health authorities, and half voluntary, including substantial backing from individual churches. All ACET's paid workers and volunteers are Christian, recruited mainly from the churches. Because of the difficult and sensitive nature of the work, ACET has to turn away more volunteers than it accepts.

It has made a major effort to try to combat ignorance and prejudice with knowledge and compassion. It has an education programme which has, so far, involved 350 schools, 50% Comprehensive, 30% Grant Maintained and Technology Colleges, and 20% private. There is a close link between the care and the education programme, so that the educators are speaking from personal contact with those who have AIDS. The volunteers for this programme usually have experience in teaching or a proven ability to communicate with children and before they go out to schools they have twelve days of teacher training, spanning three months or more.

The ACET school programmes are adapted to whatever the individual school wants, small group discussion, a forty-minute lesson or a whole day's programme. All the trained volunteers are Christians, but there is a strict rule against using their position for a Christian message. The over-riding objective is to warn of the dangers and how to avoid them. ACET go into schools on invitation and working with the head teacher or the head of department, provide a programme that will meet their particular needs.

ACET, which was founded by Patrick Dixon, then a doctor at the Charing Cross Hospital in London, keeps in close touch with the efforts to find life-prolonging drugs and especially to know the likely side-effects which may affect those under their care. The effects of combination therapies mean that people are living longer and in some cases returning to work. However the regime of maintaining combination therapy is expensive and demanding on the individual concerned. It takes a good deal of self-discipline to continue taking pills regularly over a long period of time, and sometimes they don't always work as expected.

Christian views on the morality of a promiscuous lifestyle are on the record, but Christ himself did not enquire about the causes of the ills of those hundreds whom he healed. It was enough for his great compassion that they were suffering and that he could heal them. The attitude of those who profess to follow him should be the same.

The clutches of the law

Who would be a policeman today? Long gone is the benevolent image of 'Dixon of Dock Green,' whose friendly word kept many a lad out of trouble. Today we see armed police in flack-jackets, except in the no-go estates, where we don't see them at all.

In the days of Agatha Christie, Dorothy Sayers and Ngaio Marsh, the police seemed to have plenty of time to deal with unusual and shocking events like murder and the criminals always got caught. Today the police have to choose which crimes to investigate; the rate of murder has quad-rupled and most crimes are not cleared up.

In those days there was little risk to the life of an unarmed policeman and all murderers risked their necks. Today the balance of terror is the other way. It is the policeman's life and the lives of hostages that are at risk, not that of the murderer. We can hardly wonder that the police today are a harder breed.

In Dixon's day gangsters were confined to the United States. But from the Kray gang of the Sixties, gangland killings have become part of British life. And with gangs come threats to ordinary people and graft for the police. Slowly it has dawned on us that, while most forces are clean, other forces have spots which seem never quite to be removed.

None of this has turned the general British public against the police. They are still seen by most of the public as our protection against an increasingly violent society. We'd like to see more of them around our streets. Most of us still see them as our defenders against violence and anarchy, the thin blue line which protects a civilised society.

But the murder of Stephen Lawrence reminded us that there is one group in British society which is, to put it mildly, not sure that the police is on its side. The most serious allegation against the police has been that of 'institutionalised racism.'

Hence it is noteworthy that the accusation levelled at the police during the 1985 Handsworth riots was one of 'indiscriminate arrests of black youths'. This affected the whole community. The Christian community's first response was the formation of the 'Handsworth and Aston Forum of Churches'. This was the first formal gathering involving black majority churches with other concerned Christians. By uniting in this way, exposure was given to other pressing community issues, such as poor housing, high unemployment, the level of school exclusions amongst black youths, and the strain on the black family unit due to disaffected black youths seeking their own identity and joining movements such as Rastafarianism. This identity crisis, fuelled by racism and the growing pains of an immigrant community seeking justice and self-determination, saw a community at boiling point. Through the skilful work of the forum of churches and other community groups, the heat was taken out of the situation and the community discontent reduced to a simmer.

It was nine years before this, when the church leaders at the time seemed to think hat social issues were not a 'pulpit matter', that a black pastor, Rev J Benjamin Corbett, started to think in terms of a practical gospel. This led to the founding of the United Evangelical Project, which saw its mission in terms of meeting the needs of the whole person – social, emotional, physical and spiritual. The key was a gospel framed in terms of action, and born out of a sense of justice. They had organised extra education, taken poorer children to summer camps, tried to find hostels for the homeless and had organised Black choirs, which sang as far away as Frankfurt and Berlin.

So, finding after the Handsworth riots that their sons had suddenly been swept off to some unknown police or prison cell, and believing that the police had made completely indiscriminate arrests, the parents turned instinctively to Pastor Corbett. Led by him, the Handsworth and Aston Forum of Churches insisted on seeing the Chief Constable of the West Midlands. The immediate result of the experiences of 1985 was a bipartisan black/white Christian forum working together for a better community. The long-term result was a strengthening of the work of the UEP and a plan of action called the 'Crisis Procedure', which states what action the churches would take, and when, in the event of a crisis in community relations. Fortunately it has never yet had to be used.

The Aston Legal Centre, part of the work of the UEP, is manned part-time by a group of Christian solicitors and community workers. There is one full-time solicitor, some welfare rights workers, an administrator and a group of volunteers. The work today is more about welfare rights than about keeping boys out of prison.

For example, the Home Office gave an overseas student, who suffered a kidney failure, leave to remain in Britain and a local church had found somewhere very temporary for her to live; but it was unsuitable either while she waited for a transplant or for study. Because she had a roof over her head, she was told that it would be months before the local authority could find her normal accommodation and she had also been turned down for Income Support by the Benefits Agency. She had only a disability allowance to live on and was in a very distressed state.

The Legal Centre helped her make an appeal against the refusal of income support and represented her at the Appeal Tribunal, where she was successful. Staff also went to the local Neighbourhood office and refused to leave until she was accepted as homeless. Within days she had a hostel place and, shortly after that, permanent accommodation.

The 'Prison Link' work of the Project aims to keep Black prisoners in contact with their communities and to provide their own community's style of worship in the prison. It also tries to help families to visit members in prison, wherever they are in the country. They also have a ten-week workshop at the Young Offenders Institution to try to raise their self-esteem and their aspirations and make a positive plan for their lives when their sentence ends.

There is a 'Children's network' to support young people (8-16) who suffer when a member of the family, on whom they are especially dependent, is imprisoned. Their main effort is to set up outdoor activities, such as camps and climbing expeditions, which help them to make friends with the other children and with staff and to give them the ability to develop good personal relationships.

A boy of twelve who had been attacked was going to be the central witness in a court case, and was worried about the effect of his giving evidence against his attacker. So the staff member got in touch with the Crown Prosecution Service and persuaded them not to call him in court.

Later he got into a fight at school and was excluded. The staff worker went with mother and son to see the Head, argued that his exclusion was unfair and managed to have him reinstated, since when he has done well, has come to one of the camps and seems to have found his balance.

The third and major effort of the prison work is the 'Return Programme,' partly funded by the Probation Service. It aims to sort out the returning prisoner's finances and debts, find accommodation and, if possible, a job, help them to get off drugs if necessary and to restore the link with their family.

An Asian prisoner was in arrears over housing and could not get any backdated benefit. But they found accommodation for him with Adullam Homes, who give priority to ex-prisoners.

Pastor Corbett argues that only if people feel valued will they believe that justice has been done. He believes that their non-sectarian and multi-cultural work is a practical expression of their faith and, though it is secular, they do not lose their Christian identity.

Twenty-two years after its founding, the UEP employs twenty people, providing legal and welfare rights advice, a community education pro-gramme, a youth provision including annual youth camp, the provision of safe, secure accommodation for young homeless people, a prison link service working with the prison community and their families, and a community capacity-building initiative. It attracts statutory and major grant-making trusts' funding.

The United Evangelical Project is not the only project for the Black churches, but it is clear, after the Stephen Lawrence case, that there should be more, and that other churches need to show the same solidar-ity with them that the other churches in Handsworth and Aston showed in the crisis in 1986.

3

Homes for the homeless

Down and out

Our church in the centre of Cambridge was built in the 1980s with glass doors and no steps, friendly and welcoming to everyone – including beery dropouts who came in to ask for money for 'a bite to eat,' or the urgent need of the price of a fare to Aberdeen. They were soon joined by those who had been 'returned to the community' from the mental homes, but found that no one wanted them. Some began to come to the services and to make their own vocal contribution in the middle of the sermon.

The deacons decided that we needed a policy! So all who wanted money were referred to them; the vocal ones given two warnings and then gently escorted out. And when the homeless boys started to arrive, it was decided that we would open our single back hall one evening a week. But they brought their dogs and the dogs had fleas and were not house trained and, to make way for the mothers and toddlers next morning, an army of church members was required to wash the floor with disinfectant from wall to wall. Eventually it was found that there were other older churches with lots of back halls, some of which were made over entirely to the needs of those on the street and we decided that our own new back hall was more suited to the mothers and toddlers.

Most of us find those living rough to be a bit threatening. We are used to dealing with people brought up to a norm of social behaviour and whose job requires that they behave themselves; so we are not sure how to handle those who have less self-restraint.

The Friary Drop-In Centre, Nottingham

Ann Bremner, who runs the Friary Drop-In Centre in Nottingham, seems to know nothing of these fears. She has a no-nonsense kindliness, which commands the respect of all who come to her in need of help.

She is a member of the United Reformed Church, which is not far from what used to be a hostel for the homeless and she volunteered to go and help there whenever she could. She built up a relationship with the homeless there and, since they were turned out on to the streets during the day, she saw the need for somewhere they could go. So, ten years ago, she started a drop-in centre at the church and, since the work meets a pressing need, it has gone on expanding.

The first crisis was the closure of the homeless hostel, when over a hundred people were left without a roof and the local authority could not house more than seven or eight, but Ann used her network of contacts and found rooms for the majority of them. There are, as she discovered, all kinds of reasons why people find themselves down and out.

Keith was earning £250 a week as a carpenter, but he became an alcoholic and not only lost his job, but his family relationships broke down. Then he got into debt and was evicted from his home. Because he had lived in the area for three years, the local authority housed him. The Centre has helped him furnish his flat and he is able to make friends with people who do not treat him like 'someone on the scrap-heap.' He used to work sixty to seventy hours a week and every other activity was work-related, so his great problem has been to get out of the workaholic/ alcoholic trap and fill the day. The Centre has suggested that he commit himself for a year to a programme to help children read and he feels that that has given him a springboard to get back into normal life.

Peter moved out of home a few years ago when his father said that he and his brother were fighting so much that one of them would have to go. At first he lived in a series of bed-sits, but, when he came to the Centre, Ann gave him a reference to a housing association. Being dyslexic makes it especially hard to find work, so Ann keeps him out of trouble with the law by giving him something to do with his time and he has put in for a job in the railways. Most of his friends are at the Centre and he has brought along his brother, a head chef in a local pub, with whom he has now signed a truce.

Lee gave up a job as a pot-washer in London three years ago because he found London anonymous and lonely, and got a job in a big Nottingham supermarket, but became a heavy drinker, which made him aggressive and he lost his job. He ended up in a Council house in a rough area and suffered from clinical depression. Ann got to know him and found that his accommodation was so bad that, rather than go home at night, he would stay out drinking, and was getting further into debt. So she found him a house in a different area and he began to get his debts sorted out. He told us, 'Once you're out of one cage, you're out of about six.' He was helped along by Ann's firm conviction that 'there's a way out of everything.' With a recovery in his self-esteem, he now visits people in hospital and, finding himself accepted by others, he has lost a lot of his aggression and finds it easier to mix with everyone.

Steve, too, came to the Centre because he was a heavy drinker and depressed and suicidal. Ann recommended that he go to the detox centre and he has now been able to give up alcohol. Before that his feeling was,

'If I give up the booze, I may as well give up on life.' Now, after six months off, he says that he can walk into a pub and ask for an orange juice.

When he was drinking, life just went over his head. Now it's tougher, because he has to face reality. But he respects the Centre because of its high standards and because it ignores the views of those who want to keep the needy out of the area. He respects Ann because she will not stand for bad behaviour and because she insists on seeing people through their difficulties and out the other side.

The Centre is there for those who are homeless and/or unemployed, because both can bring with them problems of personality, mental health, addiction and poverty. Ann believes that respect for the individual means that they must open the door to everyone. The only rules are that there can be no alcohol or drugs and no behaviour that offends others. Ann respects each client and treats them all as friends. When we visited them, the Friary Centre was catering for seventy men and ten women.

The Centre does its best to restore all of them to their dignity as people. Those without an address cannot get on a doctor's list and a lot of surgeries do not want 'these sort of people' in their waiting rooms. So the Centre gives them access to primary healthcare. It has a doctor twice a week and a chiropodist once a month, until they can find a permanent doctor, and a nurse and mental health worker once a week – services funded by the Council. They also have a solicitor once a week, paid for by legal aid, to advise on welfare and social benefits, marriage breakdown and consequent dispossession and on relationships with landlords.

Clothes and furniture are found by the Centre, which also helps them find training so that they can escape from dependency. It starts with 'life-skill training,' which is how to run the kind of organised and disciplined life which enables people to live and work with others. For some, this is as basic as numeracy and literacy. Some do not know such simple skills as boiling an egg or putting up curtains. Others need to know how to present themselves at an interview or how to deal with aggression – their own or other people's. And those who have been roofless need to learn how to share their lives with others. Since the Centre is a kind of club, all the members help and encourage each other. The Centre aims to be a place where people can feel safe and are both accepted and respected.

Current staffing enables the Friary Centre to be open on Mondays, Wednesdays and Fridays from 8 am until 1 pm. Usually there is free coffee or tea and a charge for rolls and, at lunch, there is soup and stew. On Sunday evening there is a fellowship evening and Ann keeps a prayer diary in which people can write down their requests. There is also a quiet time, with some teaching from the bible related to every day living. The 1989 Children's Act creates stringent responsibilities for the Centre, which means that they cannot accept children. So there is a mobile crèche in a double-decker bus, based on the Centre and staffed by two children's nurses.

Despite the public funding of specific costs, there is a large residual cost still to be met and the work also needs a team of dedicated volunteers.

The costs are about £1,500 a week, over £75,000 a year. Originally the church found funding for the project. That has now run out, but the church commitment continues. Other churches have provided some funding and the Borough Council has committed £3,000 a year for three years. In addition to running costs, about £25,000 is needed for equipment, and in the past funds have been needed for two building extensions.

Up to a third of expenditure is raised by ring-fenced grants from statutory bodies. The rest is raised by voluntary gifts, mainly from churches, but also one-off gifts from local Rotary and sports clubs, and retailers make donations of left-over goods. Donations in 1998 were £31,000.

26 volunteers from local churches staff the Centre, working on different shifts, and there is a board of trustees which oversees the whole work. In addition there has been building work, for which there were separate grants. The buildings now include showers and washing machines for clothes, which seem to be a 'must' on all such projects.

There seems to be nothing here which other churches could not do if they tried. It is true that Ann Bremner is energetic, able and wise and is fired by her Christian faith. But there are energetic, effective and wise Christians in other churches, also fired by their faith, who might well do the same.

And if government really believes that 'Welfare to Work,' will relieve the welfare budget and increase taxable income, it should see that such projects which help to get people back to work do not fail for lack of funding.

Bethany Christian Trust, Edinburgh

Not every church can keep up the initial support of their projects for the homeless. There may come a point when those who had the original vision have to decide whether to allow the project to be scaled down or develop it on their own. That is especially difficult if it is the Minister who has to decide between his church and the foundling project.

In 1981, Alan Berry was Minister of South Leith Baptist Church, just north of Edinburgh, when people with nowhere to sleep began to arrive at the church door. He suggested to the church that they buy a building on the other side of the street and, though the church was reluctant at first, it was clear two years later that something had to be done. So the church set up an independent trust with a one-off donation of £7,000 from a fund-granting charitable trust. They also earmarked the funds from the sale of a church hall and, since they could get no bank loans, most of the balance came at a high rate of interest from a loan broker.

In the two-year interval the building had been converted into a cheap hotel. This meant that the Trust did not have to face planning permission and the likely opposition of those who would object to a homeless hostel in their back yard.

For the first three years Alan Berry found it 'incredibly hard work' to start up the project and still run the church. He took leave of absence to renovate a derelict club building, using volunteers and a few outside contractors and he says that it nearly killed him. After four years he realised that he could not do both jobs. To resign from the church would mean abandoning his calling as a Minister, not to mention loss of the Manse and a regular income. But the church could find another Minister and the Trustees thought it doubtful whether the work for the homeless would go on without his vision, drive and energy. So he resigned.

When the job was complete there were 26 beds. Their first problem was that the government's housing benefit was not paid directly to the Trust, so there were heavy losses from those who, after picking up several weeks' benefit cheques, left the hostel without paying, 'doing a runner with the rent.' Since then cheques are paid directly to the supplier of accommodation. But the hostel also had to be full to pay for the high interest on the loan and, since they also provided meals, 'the days were long and the nights short.' They took whoever they could get, refugees and people who needed bread and breakfast as well as the homeless, in order to keep full. And Alan's wife and daughter had to pitch in to help.

But other help was at hand. The wife of one of the Trustees was a very good businesswoman and her skill in promotion made the need known and she was able to build up a solid list of supporters. 'Any and every contact the Trust made was added to the list.' She was also able to persuade the widening group of people that the Trust was a worthwhile charity and meeting an urgent social need. There were soon a thousand enthusiastic supporters. Just as important, the project developed a good reputation with the Housing Advice Centre who, when they had some-one who needed a bed, began to put the Bethany Trust first.

It was not long before it became clear that most of the people who came were homeless because they needed some kind of rehabilitation. Accommodation was not enough, the Trust needed someone who could sort out people's problems. Gordon Weir, a qualified social worker joined in 1990 and the Trust registered as a carer for vulnerable adults, put up a case for public funding and took over a building across the road. Gordon Weir took over responsibility for the care of alcoholics and drug addicts.

On our first visit in 1995, rehabilitation was a major part of the work of the Trust. We had just come from an alcohol rehabilitation centre north of Aberdeen. We drove about twenty miles north, then four miles down a minor road without a pub in sight, and then nearly a mile up a drive to a remote farm. Not much chance of anyone nipping out for a quick one! But Bethany Trust's rehab centre was right in the middle of town. Somehow the evident care and concern of the staff was sufficient counterweight to the temptation to go round the corner for a drink or a fix.

However it is done, rehabilitation, as we have seen, is a major effort. But those committed to help believe that it is worth all the effort to put a person back in charge of their life and to restore their dignity as a human being.

Bethany tells the story of Gavin as an example. Eighteen years of failure to cure his addiction left him a beggar on the streets, 'caring for nothing and having no desire to live.' Even when he had managed to stay sober and hold down a job as a police officer, he says that he was hiding an unbearable load of guilt. After a period in hospital, he entered the Bethany Trust's rehab unit.

He said, 'I found love, combined with a depth of understanding that I had never known before. I felt no condemnation or judgement, just acceptance. It enabled me to trust and share. The five months were painful; recovery was sometimes difficult and there were times when I felt like leaving,' but he had found a Christian faith which transformed him.

The Bethany Trust, like other Christian organisations, makes it a rule not to take advantage of the vulnerability of their clients to impose their own faith. But if an addict does find a genuine Christian faith it almost always fills the aching void left by drugs. And, if they do not find that faith, the chances are high that drugs will, once again, fill the void. Nevertheless Bethany, like the other Christian centres, stick to their rule, that they only talk of their Christian faith if asked.

Providing beds for the homeless did not need a lot of staff, but rehabilitation did. Gordon Weir's wife, Fiona, turned out to be very good both at public fund-raising and also at the heavy paperwork required for government funding for rehabilitation. But latterly only a quarter to a third has been funded by government money. Other trustees have also been helpful in raising funds and in the last few years, as people got to know about its work and as it gained their confidence, the Trust has been able to expand.

The rehabilitation work meant that people from the streets could no longer be taken into the same accommodation; so a 28 bed emergency unit was created out of a derelict tea factory and caters for 300 homeless people a year. More flats were taken to enable those coming off rehabilitation to move on to secure accommodation and another worker was taken on to look after them.

The biggest single problem in getting people out of the vicious cycle of deprivation and unemployment is to find them real paid jobs. So Bethany Trust have opened four shops in Edinburgh to sell donated goods. This gives at least some young unemployed a paid job, work experience, and training. The income from the shops' sales covers their costs, and the training leads to a Scottish vocational qualification in Warehousing or Retailing to add to a c.v. to show to future employers. The Trust also gives employment and training by doing its own maintenance and furniture renovation.

Donnie first came to the Trust to get help with his heroin addiction after coming out of prison. He started to work in one of the Bethany shops to fill his afternoons. He had helped with the family market stall in Glasgow, and knew something about selling, so he did a six month 'Training for Work' scheme and got an official level two qualification in retailing. Then he became a full-time paid employee at the shop, working on an apprenticeship, which will give him an even higher qualification. He says, 'I've been clean for a year now and I do think that this job plays its part in keeping me straight.'

The staff think he is a natural with customers and he obviously likes selling:

> 'For me, you need to enjoy what you do with your work. I get a buzz out of it. Sometimes we can turn a couple of chairs into a hundred and sixty quid and put it on the street to help people who are homeless, people who've been involved in crime and addiction and it's putting my bit back into Bethany.'

The number employed by the four shops and trained in house may seem small compared with the huge number unemployed and the Trust feel that there is more that they can do. They want to move on to the much more ambitious residential training of the nationally promoted 'Foyer' schemes, but just as they had plans and a place, the public funding on which they had depended dried up. One major Trust has now promised initial funding for three years, so they are moving ahead more slowly. But on their past record of overcoming all obstacles, they are likely to move ahead here too.

The Bethany Trust now has six levels of care,
1. Street work – a soup round with a van manned by thirty volunteers from Edinburgh churches; with night shelter in church halls during the worst of the winter.

2. Short-stay emergency resettlement in a 28 bed unit, with a maximum stay for three months while they are helped to find somewhere permanent.

3. Addiction rehabilitation for 16 men for up to nine months, then on to safe housing, before being completely off the books.

4. Safe housing, first in a shared tenancy and then on into a single tenancy. Support can include cooking, budgeting, advice on benefits and help to find training or work. Support diminishes as they find their feet.

5. Homemaking and furnishing help, based on gifts and managed through a warehouse and the shops.

6. Work creation and helping to find either jobs, education or vocational training: a scheme with a 79% success rate.

Its latest annual report shows that the Bethany Christian Trust has a turnover of about £1.5m and assets of £1m, which is not bad for fifteen years. It has the advantage of some sharp Scots businessmen as trustees who make everything count. There is no item of expenditure which does not have some income and many of the major projects have considerable offsetting income, largely from government grants. Charitable trusts produce 5% of gross income (14% of net) and donations are 17% of gross (50% of net).

But there are worries about the firmness of government funding.

Their special worry is that the Care in the Community legislation is hostile to institutional and residential care, and also that there is a low priority for the homeless and the addicted.

What they find especially difficult is the transfer of power from the Department of Social Services to local bodies. Now,

> Every client has to be funded by their home region and for many homeless people it is not clear what is their home region.
>
> When that is finally decided, someone has to take responsibility for doing the assessment and 'once a social worker agrees to do it, how soon it will happen?' Then who will process the assessment and what happens if the need is genuine, but the funds insufficient? And while this is going on . . . anything between a week and five months, the homeless person is still homeless and the addict may be in hospital, in prison or dead!

Behind all this there is the worry about the inexorable grinding down of government funds to help the helpless, covered by the rhetoric of the need for the private sector to take more responsibility.

The Bethany Christian Trust certainly takes that responsibility seriously. No one could complain that it has, in its fifteen year life, not moved in as fast as it could. It has survived the switch from government to local authority assessment of need and the quite proper hurdle of higher standards for those who take others into their care. No one could have trawled more assiduously for private funds or been more imaginative in raising money in other ways. And it is not daunted by the sheer scale of the task. But if government wants the private sector to do more than it does at present, it seems to me that they will have to be more imaginative in their own approach and develop a genuine partnership with the voluntary bodies, which have to do a very tough job.

Covering the bare boards

Down a side street in Camberwell, across the road from the railway, is an old warehouse, full to the brim with tier on tier of second or third hand furniture. The Shaftesbury Resources Centre is manned by strong young men and, when we visited, by a slight, bright-eyed girl in her mid-twenties. At first you would take her for a secretary, which is how she started four years before, but as you listened and got to know her, you would be inclined to think that she must have a Masters in Business Administration.

The business objective itself is quite simple; it is to find furniture for needy people, who will otherwise sleep on bare boards. Social services may provide the bare boards, but, too often, their new tenants do not have the money to put anything on them.

If they have been sleeping rough or if they have been transferred from a hostel, they will bring nothing with them.

– Mr Hughs had been a high-powered merchant banker, but his world had come apart. He had lost job, family and home and had spent three years on the streets. Finally a Trust had given him an empty flat, but nothing to go in it.

– Claire was sent along by the London City Mission. She had been sleeping rough for four years, but now had an unfurnished flat.

– Old Mrs George had lost every single thing through a fire in her flat.

– Mr Ali, a single parent, had lived in a hostel with his two children for eight months and the council offered a house, if he took it at once; and to help him do that they sent him along to Shaftesbury to pick what furniture he needed.

– Some just cannot replace a key item of furniture. Old Mr Zarelli's bed had finally collapsed after twenty-five years, but because he had arthritis in both legs, he needed a bed with a headboard to help him to get in and out. His local community worker sent him along.

– Some do not have the resources to provide for a growing family. The widowed Mrs Donald was left with twelve children, and the minister who came to arrange the funeral found that some of the children were sleeping on mattresses on the floor, there were no carpets and not enough drawers for their clothes and the chairs were coming to bits. So they were fitted out with carpets, some more beds, chests of drawers, a table and chairs and two three-piece suites, all paid for by the church.

In their last annual report, the Shaftesbury Resources Centre analysed the reasons why people needed help. Lone parents came top of the list with 27%, 18% were homeless, 14% refugees (a particular London problem), students and those under 25 were 16% and those who had suffered from domestic violence, 3%, leaving 20% for other or unknown reasons. 39% were black and 37% white British. Only 1% were Asian.

The lone parent issue is often secondary and the crisis is usually caused because of homelessness or domestic violence, or because they are refugees. But a single parent who wants to get out to work and has to pay for child care often does not have the money for replacement furniture or fridge. And those who have been housed without furniture need both some surplus over necessary expenses and time to build up enough savings to buy big items.

This Resources Centre, like all others, makes a nominal charge, partly to offset the costs, partly to make sure that the service is not open to abuse and, not least, to make those who benefit feel that they are doing something for themselves too. Three-piece suites cost £25, wardrobes £10 to £15, beds upwards of £12 and chests of drawers £10 to £20.

The assessment of the need is done by the registered agency which refers the client - the main referral agencies are the churches, the Citizens Advice Bureaux and the Social Services. The Resources Centre then has to assess their requests against others for urgency. The referral agency sends along a form and accepts responsibility for people turning up on time for appointments and for their ability to pay. All this is hardnosed but necessary.

The job of finding, collecting, storing and distributing large and clumsy, non-standard pieces of furniture is not easily turned into a slick operation. Yet ability to meet the pressing needs depends on speedy turnover of these bulky, space-consuming items. It is for achieving this speedy turnaround in her years in charge that Oenone Chadburn deserves especial credit. The Shaftesbury Resource Centre takes furniture from anywhere within the London's M25 beltway and distributes it mainly in the inner London boroughs south of the Thames. In four years the Centre has managed to help 11,000 people. In the last year, thirty volunteers made 4,300 van calls and shifted over 7,000 pieces of furniture in three vans. This could not have been done without highly efficient organisation.

Transport is the key resource, so a lot of thought has gone into its optimum use. They decide on one, two or three collections on a trip, depending on size and location, and, to give optimum use of the vans, loads are spread between them according to the level of access to a building as well as the length and congestion of routes. Ground floor access is the easiest, a flat on the fourth floor with no lift the hardest. Routes are planned carefully. All vans go out loaded with pieces to deliver and come back loaded with pieces that have been donated. Because of bottlenecks on the Thames bridges, no van is to be north of the Thames after lunchtime on Fridays.

The churches are a major source of donated furniture, equalled by large corporations, especially hotel groups, who dispose of furniture when it becomes out of fashion.

There are ten paid staff, including the van drivers, and thirty volunteers who help to handle the furniture. The volunteers are part young unemployed, balanced by others who are older and more experienced. It is one of the few projects we have found which can give the actual work experience needed to go on to a permanent job.

The income from the sales covers only half the costs of running the Resource Centre so, as in most projects, fund-raising is a major management activity. In the last recorded year, legacies and individual donations came to 56% of the income of £273,000 and income from companies to another 4.2%. Locally generated income, mainly from the handling charge on the furniture, came to another 18.4% and the general public gave 20%. A small remaining amount came directly from churches and Trusts.

The Resource Centre was greatly helped by an article in *The Independent* in 1992 entitled 'Victorian Charity is revived to aid the poor.' It led with the statement that, 'An Evangelical charity has revived a Victorian programme to provide food (sic) and furniture to the poor as a reply to Thatcher's changes to Social Security legislation.

The Independent's piece was especially helpful because it reported that they were looking for a larger warehouse in which to store the furniture. Someone in the Electricity Association, who read it, thought it would be a good use for a redundant warehouse to which they were tied by lease until 1998; so they donated the lease and in 1998 the Resources Centre was able to buy the building.

The Resources Centre has gone a long way since 1992, when it started with £7,000 left over from the Victorian charity, plus money for set-up costs from the Church Urban Fund. It has earned respect from a number of big companies who are only too happy to give their redundant furniture.

Among others, Hilton International have supported them, saying, 'The support and enthusiasm provided by the hard-working team at the Shaftesbury Resources Centre has enabled thousands of families and individuals in need.'

Professional managers recognise professional management.

Keeping the bailiffs at bay

In the famous Hogarth series of paintings, 'The Rake's Progress,' there is one of 'The last day in the old house,' when the gambler's debts have caught up with him and the bailiffs are in charge. Debt used to seem a very Dickensian phenomenon and out of place in the days of the welfare state, married women's property rights, and shareholder protection, not to mention full employment. If anyone was in debt it was likely to be all their own fault.

Then, in the 1980s, a huge drop in the value of houses brought the crisis of 'negative equity' and a massive repossession of homes and we were not so sure that that was just the fault of the owners. At another level, the persistent high rate of unemployment and the steady squeeze on social security have left thousands of families living on marginal incomes with debts which they find it very difficult to repay.

In a long low office, full of files, under a city centre Baptist Church, is the Bristol Debt Advice Centre, which from Mondays to Thursdays has a steady stream of visitors. They have not been on any rake's progress. Most have families and they have been living to the limit of a limited income, counting every penny. They are on low salaries or low welfare payments and make a cheap supermarket buy for five days last for seven.

Then a crisis comes along. It may be on the day that they realise that the bare weekly surplus has turned into a deficit and there is no way back. It may be that the cooker breaks down and they can't afford to mend it. So it's either expensive fast food, a diet of cornflakes and bread, or borrowing. Or the car may break down or need new tyres and they have to pay for public transport, which is more expensive than filling the car with petrol. It may be the break-up of a relationship, leaving only one income to pay for the rent, council tax and heating. For example, illness can put those living at the margin into debt and so, of course, can the loss of a job or overtime. Sometimes it is the cost of mending a leaking roof or window, with water down the wall, and children sleeping in the damp.

It's true that if debtors could adapt quickly to circumstances, like a racing driver giving a flick of the wrist to get out of trouble, they might be all right. But they had hoped that the partner might come back, that the illness would soon be over, that they could find a friend to mend the car or the cooker, or that they'd not be long in finding another job. So they borrowed to cover the gap. Even when they know that they're broke, most people don't like to admit it. It offends our self-respect, our dignity, our feeling of independence. So people are reluctant to go for advice and the first encounter at the Debt Advice Centre needs to be warm, friendly and encouraging.

'From the first instance, we were not patronised or treated as a charity case, nor were we told off; but by getting to see the whole picture we were enabled to prioritise our debts and to begin to regain control. We will never forget the question we got asked at our first meeting, 'How much do you *need* to spend on food?' We replied that we tried to live off a certain figure. They repeated, 'How much do you *need*?' We realised that we'd half starved ourselves in order not to sink, but it was still some months before we stopped feeling guilty about spending money on food.

I was desperate by the time I approached the Debt Advice Centre and was in danger of losing everything. They looked at my affairs and worked out how I could make payments to satisfy everyone. It will take me a long time to get myself straight again, but at least there is light at the end of the tunnel and I still have a roof over my head, which is more than many people can say. I'm no longer depressed and answer all my letters and telephone calls too.

You were there at the lowest point in my life. You helped when it seemed that no-one else cared or even wanted to listen.'

The Centre finds that the four most usual triggers which send debt out of control are loss of overtime, unemployment, a family crisis – for instance the loss of a partner – or long-term low income. People then take the easy way out and miss one payment and then they juggle payments on the 'chase letters' from creditors until every single creditor is chasing them. Instead of making realistic promises to repay, they promise too much and find their electricity or gas cut off and begin to get writs for repayment. At this point they turn to the loan merchants.

Loans from the bank to the creditworthy are expensive enough; but the APR for those with no credit is anything from 200% to 500% and there are loans openly advertised at over 700%, enough to double or treble the cost of a cooker even if paid back in a year; worse still, enough to put the borrower deep into a pit from which they often fear there is no exit but the bailiff's men (although this may not actually be the case).

The first job of the debt centre is to find out the full extent of the debts, then the full extent of the income and necessary outgoings – with some realistic discussion on what is necessary. Then they draw up a proposal to the creditors, which enables the debtor to pay as much as they can out of their income over a defined period. Acceptance of the proposal saves the creditor the court costs and the uncertainty of what the court would award. So mostly they settle for the proposal.

A local banker says,

It is of key importance that any repayment arrangements are realistic and therefore sustainable. The involvement of the Bristol Debt Advice Centre encourages people to be open with their creditors, which makes for better, sustainable, mutually agreed repayment schedules. Its role is very worthwhile.

The Centre has also had warm praise from local MPs. Dawn Primarolo (Bristol South, and now Paymaster General) said,

> I know from the constituents who come to my surgeries that debt can cause huge problems, not only because servicing the debt leaves no money for essentials, but also because the anxiety of trying to cope puts an enormous strain on the whole family. The Centre plays an essential role in helping people manage their debts and, as a result, they feel more in control of their own lives and finances.

And Jean Corston (Bristol East) adds,

> Anyone can get into debt at any time in their lives. It can be through losing a job, or falling prey to loan sharks. The Centre does marvellous work in enabling people to deal with debt and the stress that it brings.

Long-term, the Debt Centre believes that one of the most promising initiatives is the setting up of credit unions in the main districts of each city. All the work is voluntary, so they save the collection costs and administration of the loan businesses, so they can charge 1% a month, which is an APR of only 12.68%.

Since it started, the Centre have enlarged their office, trained workers to respond to simple cases by phone, issued a self-help guide and started visits to two of the poorest estates in the City to give outreach advice in the community to those who cannot travel. The central office is always fully booked with appointments two weeks ahead, and it wants to arrange home visits for those who are housebound, but does not have the funding available. It currently deals with well over a thousand new enquiries a year.

There is a similar debt project, the Speakeasy Advice Centre, in Roath, just to the east of Cardiff city centre. Both the Bristol and Cardiff Centres were founded by a church with a social conscience, but are independent, with their own boards of trustees.

The Cardiff Centre has two lawyers and also deals with social security matters – a refusal of help, even if only temporary, can trigger financial crisis.

A client of the Cardiff Centre had been advised by the DSS that he was not entitled to benefit, so he didn't claim it, losing a substantial sum.

When he discovered that they were wrong, the DSS argued that it was not legally responsible for its wrong advice! The Centre took up the case of Evans v DSS and the district judge found for Mr Evans. The DSS's appeal was dismissed by a senior circuit judge. The Centre believe that it was an important legal precedent, which established that the DSS was not above the law.

It may be that the DSS was driven to fight the case because of the financial principles at stake. The prolonged burden of high unemployment, combined with public insistence on lower taxes, has put a steady squeeze on the social security budget. As well as having to fight legal cases, as does any government department, its rules look increasingly mean. For those living in their own mortgaged houses, social security gives nothing towards monthly repayment of capital, and help with the interest only starts nine months after the start of a claim.

Surgery to remove a brain tumour left Mrs B disabled and in difficulties with the mortgage interest and, after ten years of struggling, she and her husband got into arrears. The building society prepared to evict them. In desperation her husband, who had only been able to obtain intermittent work in the fifteen years of his wife's illness, borrowed £1,700 from a loan company, but they signed paperwork which ostensibly created a debt of £5,500 which, inevitably, they were unable to repay. When the loan company went to court to obtain possession, the Centre took up their case and uncovered irregularities under the Consumer Credit Act, forcing the loan company to agree to reduce the debt to £1,700 and to accept payment which the couple could afford.

An Asian woman, deserted by her husband and left with four children, had never handled money and, not knowing what to do, simply relied on a few friends for food. She was, at last, persuaded by her friends to come to the Centre. After four months she was in heavy mortgage arrears and the building society was suing for possession.

The Centre represented her at court, and the court allowed her to pay the arrears over twelve years. The Centre also helped her apply for back-dated benefit to clear the mortgage and keep her home; but the Benefits Agency refused to back-date. The Centre appealed and the Appeal tribunal upheld the refusal of back-dated benefits. So the Centre appealed to the Social Security Commissioner and two and a half years after her application, the Commissioner overturned the decision and awarded her the back-dated benefit, enough to clear the mortgage arrears.

Politicians may talk about benefit fraud, and no doubt there are people smart enough to work the system. But a great many people in need do not know enough to claim what Parliament wants them to receive, let alone to work the system, and all the time it is getting harder for those in difficulties who do not know how to begin to help themselves.

Anyone claiming housing benefit has to deal with the local authority rather than the DSS, so the same person may have to handle two bureaucracies, with all the scope for confusion and error, which the claimant is seldom in a position to sort out for themselves. If that were not enough, the Social Security legislation is always being, as the politicians say, 'tightened,' but as the hard-pressed officials find, this means law and regulations being forever changed and complicated. So it often needs a legal case and a judge's decision before the contradictions in the guidelines are untangled, and a citizen's rights become clear.

Tighter budgets have also closed many Citizens Advice Bureaux and limited the service from those that are still open, so more people now come to the Speakeasy Advice Centre. Both the Bristol and the Cardiff Centres find that people in debt need time to talk through their problem and build up trust in the adviser and some are so stressed that it is hard to get a coherent story.

The total annual cost of running the Cardiff centre is £75,000, of which £20,000 comes from government's legal aid and a significant part of the balance from a donor base of seventy people, who give covenants of between £5 and £50. So fund-raising is a major activity, with presentations on the work over a free meal, to which supporters bring friends, and a video, which they show at churches. Other fund-raising projects are more spectacular. They have in the past organised a sponsored parachute jump, and a charity auction of items including the use of a stretch-limousine for a day – all in a very good cause!

4

Jobs for the Jobless

No one is unemployable

In the far north-west of Northern Ireland, beyond the Sperrin Mountains, in the historic city which the Nationalists call Derry and the Unionists Londonderry, jobs have been scarce for a long time. But, in this city of chronic unemployment, where the young may well doubt whether training for work is worth their while, a most successful training project has been set up. The Churches Trust was founded by the Methodist, Presbyterian, Roman Catholic and Anglican churches and has been heavily funded by government. It has an almost uniquely successful project in offering the unemployed experience of real jobs. Their record is that, after a year in the project, nearly half of the trainees have been able to find employment at once and most of the rest within a few months.

It is not easy for a charity to create paid jobs to do work for which they themselves receive no direct income. Even with pay somewhere between the going trades union rate and the rate of unemployment benefit, it costs a lot of money. It is also open to the criticism that it is undercutting normal business and the trades union rate for the job. And yet, if it can be done, it is immensely successful. In Northern Ireland government has, until now, thought it worth paying to help get unemployed young people off the streets. The cost of keeping troops, helicopters and armoured cars in Northern Ireland is a lot higher.

To avoid undercutting ordinary business, the project does work which could not otherwise be afforded. It helps pensioners with jobs that they can no longer do themselves and for which they cannot afford anyone else. It does public work for which the local Council can find no funds.

They have, for instance, drained the land for a sixty-acre park, planted the trees, put tarmac on the paths and put up seats. They have created a riverside walk along the west bank of the Foyle, where the old Great Northern Railway used to run to Strabane, Lisburn and Belfast. And they have removed the overgrowth from an old lovers' lane.

For the old folk, they clear the guttering, mend the washers on the taps, repaint houses, repaper rooms, tidy the back yard and front garden and do all the little DIY jobs which older people can no longer do for themselves. It all used to be free, but since cuts in government aid has been cut, they now have to make a small charge for materials – £5 for papering a room. The government cut-backs have also brought them from employing 148 people (at peak) down to 57 people and fewer staff. It is doubtful whether the 'New Deal' will reverse this trend.

Those who want jobs on the project have to make an application and go through an interview, as for any other job, and they are subject to the ordinary discipline, docking of wages for avoidable absence and dismissal for breaking the conditions of employment. The discipline works and 98% are there on time on a Monday morning. The weekly pay is £103 for thirty hours a week on the job and that gives a single person the incentive of roughly double their income on social security. They are also taught how to make applications for jobs, how to behave in an interview and how to find references. They are also given instruction on finance, health and safety at work, and personal development.

They join 'with their heads down, sure that they are worthless; but within a short time their heads are up, they feel that what they are doing is worthwhile and they have made friends. Protestants and Catholics work together and realise that the other lot are not two-headed monsters.'

The staff say that for those who have never had jobs, the first hurdle is to get out of bed in the morning, and that is where paid work has the edge on training. 'Those on the trainee schemes turn a piece of metal on a lathe and as soon as they've finished it, it's put in the bin.' But laying out a park or painting a house is making your own contribution to the real world. 'They say, "I was a part of that" and have a sense of ownership.'

Before they start, the supervisors give them a course on the equipment they will be using. From our own visit, I also had the impression that the supervisors ran a pretty tight ship and this may be one reason why local employers are happy to take their trainees on at the end of their year.

The project now has to give way before the government's 'New Deal,' which is not wage-based, but is based on social security plus an incentive subsidy to the employer. This is cheaper for the government, but the question the Churches' Trust staff ask is whether employers will be prepared to take on people who have either never experienced the discipline of work, or who have been out of the habit of work for a long time. The New Deal is also limited to six months, 'which is not enough to get the basic skills and qualifications and still leaves them on their own to find an employer.' Whether it gives teenagers not used to jumping out of bed with the alarm clock the same incentive to get up in the morning also remains to be seen. First indications are decidedly mixed.

It all comes down to political priorities. The Roosevelt Memorial in Washington, opened in 1997 by President Clinton, has stone statues of unemployed men lined up in a dole queue and set in the adjoining walls are extracts from two of Roosevelt's speeches. One says,

No country, however rich, can afford the waste of its human resources. Demoralisation caused by vast unemployment is our greatest extravagance. Morally, it is the greatest menace to our social order.

The other is his response,

I propose to create a civilian conservation corps to be used in simple work. More important however than the material gains will be the moral and spiritual value of such work.

The Conservation Corps, established in 1933 to help in the high unemployment of the great depression, enrolled three million unemployed and unmarried men between the ages of 17 and 23 on projects including reforestation and development of state parks. At its peak in 1935 it had half a million members. This Roosevelt New Deal project went on until 1942, when preparation for war brought American unemployment to an end. When the Americans finally see a problem they deal with it thoroughly!

The British government's 'New Deal' is a small but, by comparison, insufficient move in the right direction. On the positive side, it widens the income gain for those who give up social security to take on a job and it gives a cash incentive to the employer who takes on new workers. It also gives better childcare for lone parents and, as a negative incentive, tightens the rules for those who stay on benefit. It offers six-month jobs in the voluntary sector or in an 'Environmental Task Force' for projects like energy conservation, ecological management and conservation. Both these options give them a cv and would help them get a permanent job, if the permanent jobs were there. But the number of charities that can take on subsidised school leavers must be limited and it is also doubtful that there are sufficient conservation projects near areas of high unemployment organised to soak up unskilled unemployed teenagers.

What is needed is a project sufficiently strong and well organised to give back to a substantial part of the longer-term unemployed the job skill and experience which is needed to expand the employable labour force. This expansion is crucial because the shortage of experienced labour limits the Bank of England's use of interest rates to expand the whole economy. But – 'catch 22' – that expansion, in turn, is critical to the recovery of full employment.

In a lecture on 'Monetary Policy and the Labour Market,' the Bank's Deputy Governor, Mervyn King, says that the Bank base their decisions on interest rates, on the level of unemployment at which experienced labour will become so scarce as to increase inflation. The problem is that, as the rate of unemployment rises from decade to decade, the level of experienced labour gets less. In the Fifties, we had quarter of a million unemployed and little inflation. Now the headline rate of unemployment at which the Bank of England has to slam on the brakes is at best six and maybe eight times as high, one and a half to two million. (And there are many more who want to work than are in this headline figure.)

So the higher the rate of unemployment, the fewer the skills will be available at the next upturn. This is a vicious and intolerable spiral. We shouldn't blame the Bank's interest rate committee, for they are just skilled mechanics, doing a limited job within a given set of rules. We should blame the two decades of monetarist government for allowing the build-up of two million able-bodies citizens who, for lack of practice, cannot play their part in keeping our economy going. If this vicious spiral is ever to be broken, it is no good messing about at the margins. We either need projects like the Conservation Corps, adequately funded by government, or we need changes in government policy which will show a credible growth path and give companies or industries the incentives to put far more of their own money into training. And there is a powerful case for a similar project. What might it be?

The European Union have to consider further reforms of the CAP to allow for the extension of the European Union eastward and to reduce its cost to the main providers, especially Germany.

Before the first really major reform of the CAP in the early Nineties, I was founder and first chair of the European Parliament's cross-party group on CAP reform, the 'Land Use and Ford Policy Inter-Group (LUFPIG). We worked closely with the Irish Commissioner, Ray McSharry to produce the proposals which were negotiated in the Euro-pean/American deal known as the Blair House Agreement, and that deal was then locked into the world trade agreement known as the Uruguay Round in 1991.

One of our major concerns was what to do with the land which went out of production and how, if possible, to tie that in with compensation to the farmers. If nothing is done the land could return to useless and hide-ous scrub. But Europe, and especially Britain, has got used to the rural landscape produced by farming and we would hate it to go to scrub. It seemed to some of us that there was one practical alternative. With the reckless clear-cutting of so much hardwood forest around the world, we are only a generation away from a severe world shortage of hardwood. That made a strong economic and environmental case for replanting the European hardwood forests.

Ray McSharry felt that it was too hazardous to introduce other major issues into the time-table dictated by the GATT and went for the quick fix of 'setaside' which leaves land fallow. But there is now a case both at European and British levels for using this surplus land both for ecology and for the longer term resource of hardwoods and to create a conservation corps. In Britain most plantations could be within an hour's bus ride from a major city, where young people could do with a job for a year to give them the work, discipline, work experience and employment record needed to get into the labour market. If Roosevelt's Conservation Corps worked, so could ours. It could also help our Continental European partners with their much greater problem of unemployment.

The European Parliament made another proposal with rare unanimity two years later, whose time may now have come. It had already forecast that the IMF loans on offer were totally inadequate to rescue Eastern Europe from economic and political chaos. In 1993 it suggested that, since at $150bn a year, NATO's spending on cold war weaponry was a hundred times the IMF conditional offer of a £1.5bn loan, there was a strong case for converting a large part of NATO's arms industry to make civil equipment to convert Russia and Ukraine's arms industry to civil production, aimed to exploit their vast natural resources and make them into prosperous trading partners. Experts from both NATO countries and Russia gave evidence that this was feasible. While arms expenditure does not promote the growth of reciprocal trade, civil industry does and the effect of creating a prosperous Eastern Europe should be the same as the opening of the American west in the nineteenth century. The proposal was for a Marshall Plan for Eastern Europe, which made continued aid dependent on the fulfilment of the aid conditions. At the time the American administration did not respond and only now have they accepted that the results of the West's neglect are, as we forecast, so dangerous to the West that aid to Russia must be first priority. It remains to be seen whether they really mean what they say.

Meantime, the voluntary sector is doing what it can with a tiny fraction of the government's resources. For the last three years I have chaired a group of financial experts, put together by Michael Schluter of the Relationships Foundation, to try to see whether we could find a project which would enable individual cities to do something for themselves. We looked at the 'Cambridge Phenomenon,' a high-tech boom which increased employment in and around Cambridge, while all the rest of the country was going through the Thatcher slump of the early 1980s. But, for one reason or another, the 'Cambridge Phenomenon' seemed hard to reproduce elsewhere. We decided that what was needed was an imaginative initiative which would rally a whole city behind it.

What emerged was a proposal for a fund, which borrowed interest-free from the public in a city, invested in interest-bearing securities, and which used the donated interest to fund job creating ventures in the city. While our financial experts, partners in the great city firms, gave their time to making sure that the loans would be absolutely secure and to finding ways of handling and repaying the money, Michael Schluter and his team talked to the civic leaders in Sheffield, found that they were enthusiastic and were prepared to put their weight behind it. Soon there was a high-powered Sheffield board, including the Pro-Chancellor of Sheffield University, Peter Leigh. The city's two MPs in the Government, David Blunkett and Richard Caborn, held receptions and made personal pledges and other pledges rolled in from leading figures in sport and business until, by November 1999 the total was £800,000.

The Sheffield proposal is that the funds be lent to the North British Housing Association, the largest in the country and Sheffield based, for housing projects in the city and that the interest should be passed on to three local job-creating organisations in the voluntary sector.

One of these is Rebuild, a charity limited by guarantee, which has for two years built houses in the Manor estate in east Sheffield. It was set up by a local builder, Gordon Wordsworth, who had wound up his own company. Rebuild started off by putting up fifty small business units, employing three managers and local craftsmen from his old business together with unemployed young people. 80% of them were from the local city wards, where the rate of male unemployment is over 30%. Rebuild started with a work-force of 28, of which 12, including one girl, were young apprentices, most of whom had never had a job before and 6 of whom had just left school. After two years they have a work-force of 62, of which 18 are apprentices, with 10 more lent out to builders on other local sites.

Rebuild received some small grants; the Sheffield Community Development Enterprise Unit (SCEDU) gave £15,000, and, as they expanded, they had funding from the European Social Fund. They were helped by the terms of the first contract, which had a clause about local employment. Fortunately a building company does not need heavy finance; the main risk was that the new apprentices might not pick up the skills of bricklaying and carpentry fast enough for the company to cover their wages.

'Initially the commercial side saw us as community wallies in woolly jumpers,' but ten minutes with Gordon Wordsworth shows a level-headed, practical manager. He says what everyone else says, that there is nothing like hard cash for getting people out of bed in the morning and also that there is nothing like working alongside skilled brickies and chippies to train them in how the job should be done. He says that training schemes have none of this motivation and most trainees, as we've seen elsewhere, are very sceptical about finding a job at the end. They say, 'We're just being recycled.'

Rebuild pay £170 a week to start with, rising to £205, of which £83 is covered by subsidies. They have 20 weeks' paid block release at Sheffield College in the first year and 7 weeks in the second year.

'At first they see the work as a grind, but one morning, about six months out, they will come in with a new light in their eyes, keen to get on with the job.' But the proof is that, over the two years so far, they have only lost one apprentice, and he came to them both illiterate and innumerate.

The apprentices waste more materials than a skilled craftsman and the contract rates have to be 3% to 5% higher to cover that cost. The benefit is that the people on the estates do not see workers from other cities being bussed in every day to an area of high unemployment. And, 'in the longer run, since building is more labour intensive than other industries, skilled workers will always be the major bottleneck.'

Their client, the North British Housing Association, a Sheffield company, clearly takes this longer view and is prepared to pay the slightly higher price.

Another Sheffield project which will benefit from the Bond is the South Yorkshire Community Foundation, which finds money for projects in the areas of 'high deprivation', known as 'Priority 5.' Each of the dozen areas has its own Community Forum, which produces an action plan, including action to provide employment.

These projects can get matching funds from the European Social Fund for whatever they raise locally. The projects they propose must show that, in contrast to the training programmes they are creating employment.

The South Yorkshire Community Foundation see the New Deal as a pilot project for short-term jobs of up to six months. Their view is that this is not long enough and that money from the Bond will provide the vital help needed to prolong the jobs so that they do maximum good.

The third project, the Sheffield Enterprise Agency (SENTA) aims to create employment by helping people who are trying to set up small businesses and cannot raise the money commercially. Banks like enough risk capital behind their loan to look after initial losses and they far prefer to lend money to companies which already have a successful trading record.

The Enterprise Agency do not like risks either, so they make clients draw up a business plan and, if and when they are satisfied, they try to persuade the banks to come in with them. In some years they turn down more projects than they fund, in other years they fund more than they turn down and, in all, they invest about £3m a year. With bank lending on top, this amounts to quite a lot of investment and, since small businesses are quite labour-intensive, it provides a solid number of new jobs.

It has expanded steadily and, since it was set up in 1987, has given

18,000 free business counselling sessions and supported 6,500 business ventures, all of which have created jobs in the City of Sheffield.

One of SENTA's clients was Chimo, a company that wanted to rescue a small purpose-built factory, employing twelve people, which had been hit by the slump of the early Nineties. They helped with the business plan and in raising the finance, so that the employment was maintained, which for the cutlery industry at that time was an achievement in itself.

Another project was a partnership making flexible couplings for sewage and drainage, and with SENTA's help they have raised enough capital to increase employment in eleven years from two to fifty-five and have a major export business.

The third example is quite different, a beauty salon, which Catherine Millard started with help from SENTA in 1992. She has made a profit every year, has repaid the loan and now employs four people.

I did not think, to begin with, that raising large capital sums to use the interest could be the most effective way of finding funds for work-creation projects. But it clearly appealed to the civic pride of the richer citizens of Sheffield, and to many born there who had made their pile elsewhere. And it has restored to ordinary people the feeling that their city is not just in the grip of inexorable economic forces, but that they themselves can do something productive to help it. Two other cities are already interested, and if the Sheffield project works there is no doubt that they and others, seeing that something can be done, will take it up.

Finding Jobs

There is nothing that excludes a healthy citizen so completely from society as unemployment. It takes away all sense of purpose, of belonging and of hope. It is also an absurd and heavy burden on society to pay those who want a job to do nothing. Unemployment and related social security pay is the biggest single burden on the British budget, and combined with the tax revenue from getting most of the unemployed back to work, would boost the national budget by over £20bn. The only sure way to a major and lasting cut in rates of taxation is a return to the full employment we used to enjoy. If the full employment policy was abused in the past, we should correct the abuse, instead of making this generation pay so dearly for the sins of their fathers.

Those under thirty know nothing about full employment. Many of them live in inner cities or in the big post-war estates where unemployment has been as high as 50% for as long as they can remember. So they don't bother to finish at school and, even if they do, they don't bother to train for a skill or vocation. And it is the growing shortage of trained workers which, as we saw above, makes the Treasury hesitate to expand the economy and keeps us in a vicious spiral of decline. So getting the jobless into work is not only good for them, it makes it possible for government to get us out of the bind of ever growing unemployment.

None of this was in the mind of Simon Pellew ten years ago as he looked at the huge grey blocks of flats north of the bustling Peckham High Street at the height of the Lawson boom. He just thought how odd it was that there seemed to be plenty of jobs in the High Street and hundreds of jobless in the flats not so far away and wondered what he could do about it.

Being a member of a local church, the Ichthus Fellowship, he put to them a plan for active recruitment on the housing estates, and a training scheme which would help the unemployed to find a job. His church paid him a small salary, gave him an office and a computer and the Evangelical Alliance gave him £5,000 for a first trial. He then worked out a programme of training, which was awarded a grant of £12,000 over six months from the Department of the Environment North Peckham Task Force.

Their work went so well that the first grant was followed by £72,000 for twelve months from April 1990. With that, he was able to employ people to knock on doors along the bleak walkways of the flats on the big estates to find clients. This proved to be the major break-through, and changed the project from a drop-in which would give occasional help to whoever turned up, to a continuing business built on a steady stream of people coming in for training. While they also put up notices in job-centres, active recruiting of the unemployed was the key to their success and has made PECAN different from almost all other similar projects.

These impersonal and sometimes dangerous walk-ways are not the friendliest place for recruiters. It took courage to go out to knock on doors which were not usually tapped by friendly strangers. But it was the route to those who felt so marginalised that they could not go out and fend for themselves. The work now needed a much higher number of volunteers, and the backing of a large church.

When we first visited the project, in the mid-1990s, the main job was to train people to find work. Many simply needed enough self-confidence. The project employed non-professional trainers and recruiters. They treated everyone with dignity and helped to make them see that they were capable of more than they had thought possible. We were told of the newly disabled driver of heavy goods vehicles, who thought there was nothing else he could do. When asked what his hobby was, he said that he was the secretary of the Peckham tropical fish association; but, until then, he had never thought he could use that kind of skill in a paid job.

The Employment Preparation Course trains clients on how to write up a cv, to fill in application forms, to answer questions at an interview and, especially, how to make the best of themselves. From the beginning the project has had a success rate of over 70% either in finding people jobs or in getting them into full-time training.

Ages range from 16 to 60, but most are in their late twenties or early thirties. Of the over 50s more than half go on to find work or training. The age range helps the under 25s on the New Deal programme to have a taste of what it will be like to work with people who are older and who come from very different backgrounds. It also gives them confidence that they can relate easily to older people.

Over the last five years PECAN has widened the range of help it can offer, and is now giving specialist courses, one on computer skills.

Uzi knew that she would have to have computer skills to work for an airline. She said, 'I panicked when I first started the course; I didn't know anything, but the teachers make everything seem simple.'

Kingsley wanted a better job and new skills. 'If you don't have computer skills, no office will want you.' He wanted to go on to work in finance and the course gave him a stepping stone.

There are others, many of them single mothers and many immigrants who have the far more fundamental problem that they are not literate, and they are offered a one-to one course.

Yemi's first child was just starting school, 'so I need to learn so that I can help *her* to learn.'

Logan, aged 41 had disguised his problem and pretended that he could write. It took courage to own up, but, when he lost his job he came to PECAN and said, 'I wish I'd done it years ago.'

They were able to help George, who had had a head injury and couldn't remember how to read or write.

Then, in inner London, there are many whose main handicap is that they cannot speak English.

Alexandra from Bogota said, 'In my last school, they just followed the text-book, whether you understood each lesson or not. Here they know how to explain things so that I can completely understand.'

The courses are recognised by Woolwich College, so that even the simplest courses are given some accreditation.

PECAN now has 48 staff. All staff are paid at the same rate, £15,000 for full-time staff and pro rata for part-timers, so that there are no salary complications in their changing jobs. More staff enable more people to be helped and with the ever-increasing number of projects the annual turnover for this coming year is likely to be over £1m.

Simon Pellew argues that it could not have expanded at this rate if he had not drawn up the carefully thought out plan of operation, which guided them. He says that too many voluntary projects go on from hand to mouth without thinking through what they are doing and why, and then going on to get agreement from all concerned on the resulting guidelines by which they have to work.

He says that he was saved from thoughtless over-confidence by making one bad mistake early on, when he opened a launderette on one of the big blocks of flats. He was so full of early enthusiasm that he did not believe the survey that cast doubt on the demand and he was careless in the security precautions. It cost PECAN £8,000, which was a lot of money early on, but it brought him up short and made him think long and hard at every new step. His church kept their nerve and decided that despite the loss, the project should go on.

Ten years ago, the Southwark Borough Council was hostile to the church's playing any part in the social needs of the community. Now it is an active and helpful partner and much of the work of PECAN is run with public finance.

The sources of funding for 1998 were,

Borough of Southwark	£137,765
European Social Fund	£57,732
Further Education Funding Council	£89,351
Other statutory	£12,227

In theory PECAN could be replicated anywhere. In practice it has so far depended heavily on the enormous enthusiasm, drive and ability of one man, and the backing of a church which is more dedicated to social action than most and has not only found funds but has actively encouraged its younger members to take part. But there is no reason why others should not do the same and projects, once started, do tend to attract the kind of people which they need.

Simon Pellew says that the project, like most small businesses, is only as good as the next big cheque, and he feels that they are never more than two weeks from the edge. So the project needs professional funders, who know what the donors want. Trusts look for innovation and, in picking up new ideas, find it more comfortable to move in the same direction, so they tend to change fashion together. Business looks for commercially minded projects. Government wants projects that are safe from political trouble as well as successful.

The smallest things can put donors off, the wrong letterheading, delay in answering the phone; the more so because it is extremely hard to measure tangible outcomes from charitable projects. So professional fundraisers have to have their ears to the ground and reshape the image of the project in accordance with changing ideas. And it is fatal to pick fights with donors over secondary issues!

He has found it essential, even in a project small by comparison with business, to be professional both in accounting and in security. Early on they lost too much money through vandalism, theft and poor staffing. And the demands of public donors are rising. The New Deal, the European Social Fund (ESF) and the Single Regeneration Budget are gradually merging and to get money out of them – especially out of the ESF – is becoming increasingly complex.

I agree with him: when I was MEP for Cambridgeshire, I tried to look after the Cambridge Women's Resources Centre. They did a wonderful job, especially in training women who wanted to come back to work after having families. They were full of enthusiasm, but I was forever being called in as they ran late with the boring job of sending in applications to the ESF. MEPs are so belittled in Britain that they are too seldom asked to cut through the red tape of Brussels. But MEPs are the only people to whom the European Commissioners are publicly responsible and who can make or break the public reputation on which their political future depends. So projects looking for funds from Brussels should remember that Commissioners do not normally let their staff stand needlessly in the way of a determined MEP. And with the dismissal, in Spring 1999, of the entire Commission, the influence of MEPs should be even greater!

As PECAN grew, all kinds of other problems arose. It was no longer possible to rely on one church alone, there had to be the network of local churches, which now supports PECAN. They then had to decide what to do to keep the Christian vision, as the day-to-day focus became the efficient management of a training business. Simon Pellew feels that it needs a strong board of trustees, which he has, to make sure that the managers keep their Christian focus.

He himself believes that if the aim of Christian social action is to be an expression of God's love, then Christian values must be embodied in the relationship between all the members of staff and, externally, between the staff and all those they deal with. He believes that it is also essential that not just the managers but all the staff should be Christians, since there should be equal opportunities for every employee. That does not prevent the project sub-contracting specialised work to secular organisations. But if the direct employers are all to be Christians, the project needs to be able to draw on a wide group of churches. And since the whole business is one of personal relations and trust, staff have to be trusted by the clients and personally approachable.

I have met other people of Simon Pellew's talents, his useful and attractive mixture of self-doubt and determination. Most of the other people have already made a fortune, but Simon Pellew's fortune is laid up in a safer place.

5

Churches in the Community

The Bridge Chapel, Garston, Liverpool

The lady in the front row at the opening of the church's new community centre looked tired and strained. She wore the chain of office of the Lord Mayor of Liverpool and this was just another project in her daily round of engagements thought worthy of civic encouragement. Afterwards she would go straight on to the next.

But afterwards the gleaming mayoral limousine sat outside waiting. The church's community centre had really gripped her and she insisted on staying to see meet all those involved. The singing of the group of adults with learning disabilities stood out, both to her and to the rest of us. They were the sort of people usually seen blank-faced and hand in hand with a harassed carer. But the church's group were all dressed in their best clothes, their hair well brushed, eyes bright, faces beaming, and their singing really good. At the end one of the men, bursting with pride, came to give the Lord Mayor a present from the church. She not only stayed on that afternoon, she asked all the group to Liverpool City Hall and made each sit in her gilt chair and wear her mayoral chain!

Garston Bridge Chapel had started under the shadow of the dual carriageway that runs past Garston docks, up the Mersey south-east of Liverpool. Their first outreach was a coffee-shop, The Open Door, on the main street opposite the super-market. A church member gave up his professional job to become the manager and ran it with volunteers from Bridge Chapel. The volunteers don't fuss the customers, but are friendly people and easy to talk to. For those who want it, there is also a Christian bookshop upstairs.

As the rate of crime and drug addiction rose and families began to break up, the needs around them struck the consciences of the church. The chapel was used for a drug counselling centre, a parents and toddlers group (specially helpful for single mothers), a drop-in centre for anyone in need (at which a low-cost meal for thirty people was provided every Friday), and also for clubs for teenagers and children.

Then the church outgrew its building and began to use a school assembly hall a mile up the hill in Allerton. The congregation continued to grow until it filled the big school hall each Sunday. Then, suddenly, the City Council decided to merge two schools and to sell for housing development the school buildings the church was using. The church asked the Council whether they could buy the buildings and the playground for parking, and on the basis of a valuation suggested a price of £275,000, with 10% down in cash within a month, terms which most churches would find it hard to meet.

The church knew that they would need to find double that amount to convert the buildings, but they wanted to go ahead. So they decided to ask for pledges and were confirmed in their determination when members and friends pledged £500,000, which covered both the price and a large part of the conversion costs. At the opening a year later, almost all the essential costs had been covered.

The elders felt that the main reasons for this prompt response were that two thirds of the congregation were new Christians, with a strong sympathy for the pressing needs of their friends and neighbours. This was reinforced by the church's teaching that Christians have to work out their faith in practical ways. No appeals are made for money, but the church's annual income is £100,000.

So when the crisis came and they had to decide whether to buy the school, their strong calling to care for their neighbours was already there. They could see, not only how much more room they would have for the current social projects at the old chapel, but how they could expand to meet other pressing needs as well.

There's more room now for the parents and toddler's group, where fifty come on three days a week. The local divorce rate has risen by six times in the last few years and a great many of the group are single parent mothers, some as young as 14 and 15. They have a very low self-worth and the great need is to build their confidence. A minority also need to come off drugs. There is also a counselling service, dealing with a variety of people and the problems they face. As we left, a pretty teenage girl arrived for counselling. She was pregnant as a result of being raped, and, against the wishes of all her family, did not want an abortion.

There is also an eight-week divorce-recovery workshop, run by Christians who have suffered the trauma of divorce, who try to befriend the newly-divorced and help them to come to terms with separation. Because of the degree of violence and robbery, the church houses a branch of the national 'victim support scheme' with two full-time workers and twelve volunteers to give moral and practical help to a constant flow of traumatised victims.

The renovation of the old building has enabled the church to fit in half a dozen bedrooms for temporary housing for the homeless and they are trying to find an experienced Christian group to look after it for them. They also want to renovate an area for work training, an after-schools club, a day nursery and a drop-in centre and to expand their work for those with special needs. And when the old playground is resurfaced, they want to use it for outdoor sports.

There is no heavy supervision of those engaged in social work. The church recognises their gifts and lets them get on with it. They believe that ministry matters more than buildings and that they need to have three or four full time paid staff; but they still aim to find enough money to finish the building work. One or two of the staff have been in the local social services, with whom the church has easy relations.

There is a part-time caretaker, who took us round the district, explaining that though the houses looked as neat as they had done when they were built, the stresses and strains of life inside were quite different. We drove past a pub and he said,

> Some kids were damaging a BMW parked outside and the owner came out and told them to clear off. They attacked him and killed him. Then they cleared off.

We didn't think that they would have taken on the chapel's caretaker; he was heavy and strong enough to keep any vandals away. But nor would there be much hostility. The district knows the chapel is there to help.

This may leave the rest of us feeling a bit overwhelmed and also wondering whether all this effort affects the work of the church for their own members. We were assured that the preaching and teaching ministry of the church goes on, with classes for 200 young people, adult bible classes, house groups, a hospital ministry and prayer meetings.

But the church has, very sensibly, put the social outreach under a Trust, with a manager who answers to the trustees. The full-time and voluntary workers are accountable to the manager and not to the minister, so the minister is not put in the impossible position of being both boss to the volunteers as well as their pastor. But the projects are rooted in the teaching that those who follow Christ should care for their neighbours as he did for his.

There must, in all such great work, be a moving spirit. Bill Bygroves has been Pastor since the church was in Garston and, though he would stoutly deny it, what has happened must be due, to a large extent, to his dedication and vision; also to his ability to put together a first-class team and then to let them have their heads. Above all, he has inspired the church with his vision and, through all the ups and downs, has carried it with him. It may also help the local relations of the church that he once played for Liverpool, is a coach of their junior team, and keeps a football in his vestry. It takes all sorts in the ministry.

West Street Baptist Church, Crewe

Oh mister porter, what shall I do?
I wanted to go to Birmingham
But they put me off at Crewe.

In their heyday, before the motorways and jet engines took over, the railways linked one end of Britain to the other and the hub of the whole system was the great railway junction at Crewe. Boat trains went through to the Dublin ferry at Holyhead and to the Belfast ferries at Heysham and Stranraer. Expresses from Glasgow, Liverpool and Manchester went south for London Euston and for Birmingham (where the little lady of the music-halls wanted to go) and there was a pretty line through the Welsh borders to Cardiff and Swansea, on which I travelled back from a scout camp on the Gower in 1939. All the lines are still open, but the crowds have gone.

Crewe still has the factory which makes Rolls-Royce cars, now owned by a German company, but the great railway workshops behind the high blank walls along the far end of West Street, which were the heart of Crewe's economy and employed eleven thousand are nearly derelict. Today's much smaller modern building employs only a thousand.

At the near end of West Street the Baptist church was, until a few years ago, on its own way to dereliction. A visiting preacher was startled by the appearance of a rat from a hole in the floor and he watched out of the corner of his eye it as it strolled down the side of the church and disappeared down another hole. As older members died off, the congregation of the once thriving church came down to 100, and less than half that number present on a Sunday.

Yet, in the last twenty years, it has invested over £500,000 in new floors, in decoration of the service area, with comfortable chairs instead of pews, in building a four-window bookshop in place of the heavy front door, in modernising the outer halls and in adding to them a new upper storey. It has also turned a butcher's shop next door into a coffee shop serving light meals throughout the day. The aim of all this work was to make the church more accessible to their neighbours in the small brick houses fronting on to West Street and to all who pass by.

That this small church has pulled itself up by its bootstraps is all the more remarkable, because West Street is at the working class end of Crewe and the membership is not rich. But they saw the need around them and, somehow, they found the money.

Geoffrey Willetts, who has been the Minister during this time of change, puts its beginning at a time of prayer which he had with an elderly

Pentecostal couple, after which, he says simply, 'things changed'. He began to look at his church with different eyes and to see that it was in danger of becoming an 'irrelevant antiquarian society.' All through the week, when people were bustling up and down West Street, the big heavy Victorian doors at the top of the church steps were barred, as if the church was a fort where the faithful few were hiding from a wicked world. And on Sunday, when they were briefly open, the little shops all around were shut and the street was dead.

One of their first decisions was to make the word of God accessible by changing their seventeenth-century Authorised Version of the Bible for the clarity of the twentieth-century New International Version and changing the form of service to a much more lively worship in song and prayer.

Geoffrey Willetts also concentrated on the kind of teaching and prayer which led directly to action on behalf of others and not just to a 'feel-good factor' for the hearers themselves.

The first big project was to put the bookshop in the place of the closed Victorian doors, its windows and lights showing passers by and those waiting at the bus stop outside, that the church was alive and part of the street. To pay for this they had their first gift-day, asking, not just for what people could afford on that day, but for pledges for the future. The congregation of 150 raised £42,000, an average of nearly £300 per member.

This generosity did not come out of the blue. Geoffrey Willetts taught that it was the duty of all Christians to tithe their pre-tax income and, before the gift-day, they also had prayer meetings every day for a month from twelve to one o'clock and from six to seven in the evening.

They set high standards for the bookshop and this paid off because, with no other Christian bookshop in a fifteen-mile radius, they sell Sunday School and Alpha Course packs as well as books to other churches too. For the local trade they have greetings cards and a photo-copying service. The bookshop is run by two part-time managers and four voluntary workers from the church, and it pays its way.

The second project was the coffee-shop in a converted butcher's shop on the street-front alongside the bookshop. The butcher's shop cost £10,000 and the cash for a quick sale was borrowed from the bank and quickly repaid. The big cost was the kitchen equipment and the furnishing, which came to £65,000.

At first the cafe was known on the street as 'the Jesus shop' and was said to be 'too nice for the area.' But, being by the bus stop, local people soon started to use it. By now the use is about half from the church and half from outsiders, many of whom are office workers in the area. It serves coffee and tea and hot lunches from a limited menu.

It is also used by those who want help from the church and who find a chat over a cup of coffee far less intimidating than an interview in the minister's vestry. The church uses it to feed those who come to the church in dire straits – for instance those who have to wait over-long for money from social services and meantime have nothing to live on.

Since the cafe, like the church, is in a rough district, with drug-dealing not far away, the mainly female staff have a 'panic-button' if they need immediate help and there are security shutters in both bookshop and cafe. From time to time mentally difficult people come in, but they seem to calm down as the Christians in the cafe pray for them. In one especially difficult case, a man was rebuked 'in the name of Jesus' and became quiet at once. So, in one way or another, the staff have been able to handle all difficult cases.

The cafe is labour-intensive, has four paid staff and runs at a loss of £6,000 a year; but there is no doubt about its use as a bridge between the church and the neighbourhood.

The third project was the modernisation of the main church building. Anyone who sat on the old pews in a velvet coat would leave half the velvet behind. The pews had to go. There was wet rot and dry rot in the timbers and a large section of the floor was held together by the pews nailed in across it. So there had to be a new floor and the space below was filled with 90 tons of hardcore. When the floor was in, the pews were replaced by moveable and upholstered chairs.

The whole cost was £50,000 and there was some complaint that the church was spending on buildings and not on people. But, so long as the church was seen as a mission to people rather than a club, it really was an expenditure on people. A lot of the members donated a chair, which cost £32.

It was then decided to modernise and equip the space in the side halls for 'mothers and toddlers' and other outreach projects, which would cost £310,000, the most expensive expansion so far. It was said that this was just too much and that it couldn't be done. But, on a third gift day, gifts and pledges of £92,000 came from ordinary members of the church, teachers and office workers.

The Mothers and Toddlers group was started by a few grandmothers, who brought along old toys on one day a week. Then young mothers volunteered and brought added freshness, enthusiasm, ideas and equipment. Nurses and health service visitors who attended the church fed in new members. The group charge 70p a session. Five people are paid by the church at a cost of £12,500 a year and are supported by unpaid volunteers who help with tea and coffee.

About 250 mothers use the group, and the staff pray with mothers about their problems. Four have now started to come to the Sunday morning services. The majority are single mothers, but some fathers and grandparents come too. The group complies with legal standards and is on the police computer.

There is an additional project, specifically to support single mothers, run by three members of the church. They give advice on social services and other help available.

The buildings are used by other groups. They include a group of mentally disabled people, cheerful and non-threatening. One of them is happy in scanning the magazines at about a page a second and then starting all over again. Another simply wants a pile of paper, which he tears up sheet by sheet.

They did at one time provide rooms for a Training for Work project, funded by the local TEC and run by two cheerful teachers who could normally be trusted to get work out of the most indolent. But the people they were trying to teach were there because it was a condition of their social benefit. So they were far less motivated than those taught by PECAN and other such projects, who desperately wanted jobs. With all the teaching, energy and enthusiasm, few of them saw the point of the basic discipline which employers needed.

There is a youth group for about seventy teenagers in the church on Sunday nights and a housegroup for young people with music on Tuesday nights. To reach out into the area there is a youth group on Friday nights with coffee and games in a shop down the road and the group has its own football team. Finally, there is an art class for about half a dozen whose teacher was a bitter political activist before he became a Christian and now wants to use his talent for the church.

None of this activity has diverted the church from its duty to preach the gospel and to teach the faithful. The church has now grown from 150 to 250 and is still growing. Their view is that the preaching of the word and concern for our neighbour are both obligations which have been commanded by Christ and the Apostles, and we cannot choose to do one and not the other.

The King's Centre, Chessington

If there is still a 'Bible Belt' in Britain, it is probably in the outer London suburbs like Chessington, which sprawls between the Kingston By-pass and the Zoo on the Leatherhead Road. Its neat suburban houses, each with their garden and garage, are a long way from West Street Crewe and Garston docks.

But it has troubles enough. A noise outside brought Trevor Archer, the church's joint pastor, to the window to see a woman screaming at her little son as she kicked him down the road. All was not well behind the bright paint and cheerful curtains. He and others in the church felt, with increasing strength, their duty to give practical help to those around them.

In the early 1990s Chessington Evangelical Church had already begun to give support to those on the fringes of society who came to the church for help. The most organised form of help was a mother's and toddler's group, of which nearly a third came from outside the church. Then, when the church outgrew its buildings and had to move to a school hall, that helped the youth work to expand and to bring in more outsiders. Members of the church also began to help in schools by taking assemblies and by supporting the local schools worker (also a member of the church) in discussing ethical, social and moral issues with groups of pupils. And the church began to build up a good reputation in the Borough.

As a result of their reputation, they were unexpectedly given the chance of a huge new involvement in the local community. Between the western fringe of Chessington and the A3 lay land which the RAF no longer wanted and which was planned for housing, subject to two acres for community use. One acre was scheduled for a sports hall; the other was offered to the church.

The church leaders felt that this fitted in with their increasing conviction that they needed to be far more involved in meeting the needs around them and, with great boldness, they suggested that they take over both acres and incorporate the sports hall into a recreational, community and church centre in the same building. They put their reputation to the test, and their offer appealed to the Borough.

The cost of their contribution would be £1.5 million. They were a comparatively small church, with about 140 members, with an annual income of £130,000, and £250,000 in reserves. But the elders felt that, if society was turning to the church, it was up to the church to take risks.

They dipped one toe into the water to spend £20,000 for a professional report on the viability of the scheme and the report gave them something practical to work on. They decided that the only realistic way of running the complex was for the church to take responsibility for the centre as well as the church and, just to make sure that they safeguard the church's identity, they incorporated the church's basis of faith in the proposed agreement. To all of this the Borough agreed.

Then came the crunch. The tenders came in from the contractors and they had finally to commit themselves to the ultimate expenditure of £1.5 million. They had the £500,000 in the bank from the reserves and the sale of the old church building. They raised £600,000 in cash, pledges and covenants from the church membership. Though some help came from Christian trusts and other churches, they were still short of £250,000, which they borrowed on the personal guarantees of the elders.

Then they had to face the job of running the centre and to learn that running a business is not the same as running a church. They were greatly helped by having Bob Robinson, a young, practical and energetic professional engineer, a member of the church, who was seconded for two years by his company, Brown and Root, to take charge of the operation.

The community activities in the Centre pay for its running costs, including the reimbursement of salaries, and there is enough left over to put aside for future maintenance. So the capital put in by the Borough in the form of the 'developers' contribution' has given them an outstanding building.

There is a large entrance hall with a pleasant cafe and on the left is the huge hall which is used for sports, exhibitions and conferences during the week and for the services on Sunday. On the right is a complex of warm and bright rooms, which are used both for community and church activities and upstairs are the offices used for the church.

The centre is used by Kingston University for examinations, and on regular days of the week for five a side football, badminton and netball, and also for major arts and education events. The smaller rooms are used for business conferences, aerobics classes and a creche.

The church has tried to allow its own activities to grow naturally rather than to rush ahead just because it has the space. But they seem to have grown rapidly all the same, especially in the help given to refugees and others from oversees who look for friendly faces to help them with their problems.

Two church members with children in primary schools started to meet Korean mothers for coffee once a week. This has expanded into meetings with international women every Friday and there is also a programme of social events for 'Amigos' with nearly forty names on the list.

Mothers, not able to read English handwriting ask their church friends to translate their children's school reports. While their mother was back in Japan at her grandmother's funeral they looked in most days on two Japanese teenagers in case they needed help. They helped a Korean girl who had crashed her car to get it to a garage and to deal with the insurance. They are also beginning to help the rising number of new refugees, though they find that the barriers of culture and language are far higher than with the overseas wives.

The mother's and toddlers group has grown much larger and now has 120 mothers and a waiting list. Members can come once a week and the group is run twice a week. They have begun social evenings with a meal and a speaker, dealing with issues like stress in the family, family values and the meaning of Christmas. The mothers now know each other and have begun to help each other and to go on holidays together.

They now have a parenting class, which runs for twelve weeks, where only about a quarter are regular churchgoers. They deal with discipline, children's self-esteem and rivalry. The class aims to help those who want to improve their skills as parents and takes great care not to be judgmental. One husband said that his wife had found real friendship at the centre and that she had been able to stop taking anti-depressants.

The church is clear that it is not dealing with the worst cases of social breakdown, but believes that it is not easy to deal with cases of real social breakdown alongside the care of those who want to make sure that it doesn't happen to them. For instance none of the five cases referred to the parenting class by the Social Services lasted the course, because the class made them feel even more alienated and powerless. Prevention is better than cure and clearly there is a place for helping people before real damage is done, when their case would be far harder and the help needed much more intensive.

The plunge in at the deep end has brought home to the Chessington church more suddenly perhaps than to Garston or Crewe that organising help in the community is very different from running a church. You cannot have a Minister who is at one moment a pastor giving advice and the next minute a boss giving orders. So in Chessington, as elsewhere, the two functions have been kept distinct.

And Chessington's swift plunge into its new work soon ran into the practical limit of spare-time activity for those who also had to care for a young family and to work for a living. The church learnt that it had to plan its activities within the sustainable limits of voluntary workers. But as the very real stresses and strains were overcome, the work made for far stronger friendships and a great camaraderie.

It also learnt quickly that, when dealing with families, there were a host of public regulations which had to be known and kept; that there was no point in duplicating what was already done in the public sector and elsewhere; and that, most important of all, the church needed to do some research into the real needs of the area.

What is especially encouraging in Chessington is the partnership between the church and the borough. Not only was the partnership in setting up the community centre encouraging, so is the continuing involvement of the borough. It is represented on the user's committee of the Centre, and the Centre's first Manager, Bob Robinson, used to sit on one of its family support forums. The Centre is working with the borough's youth services on the problems of street children and the borough's adult education department have suggested that the Centre set up activities for refugees. It has a borough grant for its parenting classes.

None of this has in the least detracted from its autonomy as a church. The main effect on the church is that a great many more people know that it is there, appreciate what it is doing and accept it as an integral part of the community. And, apart from all the practical help which the church gives to its neighbours in need, it is an enormous step forward that a Christian church, instead of being so far on the margins as to be nearly invisible, is now seen to be central to its community.

6

City Networks

By the beginning of the 1990s, it was clear that the country's social compassion had begun to dry up. In the election of 1992, the Labour Party, still standing for the policies of the welfare state, was defeated for the fourth time in succession and the frank statement of John Smith, the shadow chancellor, that taxes might have to be raised, took the blame. Labour decided that it would not be able to return to office without a change of policy. So the numbers of needy people who knock on church doors would go on increasing.

In that year I was elected as President of the Evangelical Alliance, which represents three thousand churches with about a million members. The Alliance hoped that I would not see this as simply a titular job, but could get actively involved in one way or another. As we talked about it, it seemed to me that the best use of time and energy was to help churches see how they might deal with the new demands from the rising number of people in need who, because of the steady squeeze on public welfare, were looking to the church for help. At the first meeting I attended the Alliance's Council gave their warm support.

In my four years as Chairman of the British Overseas Trade Board, I had found that exporters were fed up with government exhortation and we decided that the best way of promoting exports was by looking at practical examples. On each of fifteen city visits, starting in Sheffield and ending in Belfast, we asked four successful local export companies to tell us in some detail, with the help of audio-visuals, the basis of their achievement. We had about five hundred at each conference and the local press gave wide coverage to the successful companies. And, whether we had anything to do with it or not, the rise in national exports in those four years, 1975-79, has never been equalled since!

So I thought that it would be helpful to follow the pattern of city visits and of building on the existing social projects of the churches in each city. I thought that it would also be helpful to find a simple way in which anyone who came to the church door in need could be directed to a place where they could find help.

In my last year as a member of the European Parliament, with our mandate running out and colleagues preparing for the 1994 election, I started on the city visits, greatly helped by Chris East and Rachel Westall of the Alliance. The Alliance churches covered every kind of Protestant denomination, from the national Churches of England and Scotland to the most recently arrived charismatic 'Community Churches'. The first responses from church leaders were encouraging.

We suggested that churches form a network of social projects in their city, issue a directory to tell every church what and where these projects could be found, appoint a steering group of experienced lay people to help develop the network, and, at a suitable stage, have a public launch to let the city, and especially the social services, know that the network was up and running.

I was also asked to speak at the six Spring Harvest and Word Alive Easter conferences and the average audience at each seminar was about a thousand. My parliamentary colleagues, who were hard put to it to get twenty to a political meeting, found this incredible. But it showed that there was real anxiety about the state of the nation among the churches and that they welcomed a practical proposal that enabled them to do something about it.

In the five years since then, we must have visited once or more twenty five to thirty cities (or London boroughs) to meet church leaders and church projects – and there are visits still to come. So far there are seventeen new networks and in five more cities, church leaders have agreed that they should be set up.

The seventeen are in Aberdeen, Edinburg, Sheffield, Liverpool, Manchester, Nottingham, Coventry, Worcester, Swansea, Cardiff, Bristol, Hackney, Havering, Lewisham, Eastbourne, Brighton and Southampton. There is no single pattern for a start-up, since each city is different as is the composition of the churches. But the main objective is to get the backing of the churches and for make sure that those with most resources help more with least.

Sheffield is a major city with a population of over half a million and, because it stands well outside the West Yorkshire conurbation, it has a culture and identity all of its own. It has a proud tradition of specialised steel and its own city livery company with its splendid 'Cutler's Hall.' Today its prosperity has been gutted and three foreign-owned automated works now turn out the specialised steel which used to give the city its main employment.

Philip Hacking, the Vicar of the big Anglican church in the prosperous suburb of Fulwood, hosted the meeting for church leaders at which they decided to set up a network. His church asked a retired civil servant to be secretary and found another vicar to chair a steering group.

The Sheffield steering group then decided that they ought to include the whole of South Yorkshire, so that their network now covers a population of over a million. The directory not only shows what is being done; comparison with other directories has been found to highlight what is missing. As a result they hosted the initial meeting for the Relationships Foundation which resulted in the employment bond project described in the chapter above.

The city of Manchester is twice the size of Sheffield and it took a good deal longer before the Manchester Network was finally launched. Manchester's rich suburbs are in the south and its poverty is mostly in the centre and north. The gulf between seemed wide and deep. Those engaged in the many projects were, of course, very enthusiastic; but we felt that we had to stick to the object of the exercise here as elsewhere, which was a Network which would be owned by the churches, who, between them, would take responsibility for its success.

We made four all-day visits, two minor ones, spoke at a Lord Mayor's breakfast and at two prayer meetings with five hundred people before Manchester Christian Action Network was launched at a third packed prayer meeting, our name spelt out in full to avoid confusion with its convenors, also called 'Network,' which was chaired by a patient retired engineer. He had helped us through all the problems and then agreed to chair our new steering group. This last prayer meeting was on social action; the Bishop of Manchester also spoke and the final inspiration was an uninhibited Canadian woman, who was the Salvation Army's commandant for the North East.

Fifty leaders of a dozen projects in Manchester came up to the front to explain what they were doing and we felt that this meeting of the churches and projects was a great beginning.

In London, we would have liked to work by the four quadrants, north-east, south-east, south-west and north-west. This would have brought rich and poor areas into one network. But there was as much objection from the poorer boroughs as there was from the richer. 'Those people out there don't understand double deprivation!' And the civic identity of each borough was surprisingly strong and each was as big as a small city. We have visited six boroughs and, so far, three have a network.

In some cities, Glasgow, Liverpool, Belfast and Swansea, networks were all set to start when the key local church leader, who had held all the strings, was posted elsewhere, the net unravelled and had to start all over again.

In one small city, Worcester, there was already a network, 'Jesus in the City' and they asked us to lead a public launch, which packed the biggest church in the city centre. In Nottingham there was already a directory of local projects and we have used that as a prototype for all the others.

We suggested to church leaders that it was vital that they took ownership of the network but that they delegate the care of it to a group of about half a dozen experienced lay people. This pattern seems to work well, though there was usually one person who is the driving force. In Coventry and Southampton it was the director of the City Mission; in the two London boroughs of Havering and Hackney it was the Vicar of a large Anglican church; in Nottingham the young staff worker in a big Pentecostal church who compiled the first directory.

Keeping the ownership of the networks in the hands of the churches and the steering groups responsible to them helps the church members to feel a reciprocal responsibility to support the Network and its separate projects. Clearly, a directory of projects has to include all the projects in a city, whether they are sponsored by churches in the network or not. And when there are desperate needs, the social services and all the church projects have to work together. However much the social services may struggle to keep their secular identity, when push comes to shove, they do not turn down Christian volunteers who are able and willing to help. And the more churches and social services help each other, the more a mutual trust and spirit of partnership build up.

That partnership can be helped by a public launch of the network. The Lord Mayor elect spoke at the public launch in Sheffield and urged a close co-operation with the social services. In Southampton the social services came to the public meeting and the steering group reported a much better relationship from then on. In Worcester the public launch brought front-page headlines, 'From Pulpit to Pavement' and a very strong endorsement. The Mayor of Brighton and Hove launched their Network.

The new networks are still finding their feet, but already have useful experiences, which are worth passing on. So this section describes three: Nottingham, Southampton, and the London Borough of Hackney.

Nottingham

The city has a population of 384,00, the largest in the East Midlands, and an excellent university. But, like other cities its main industries have been hard hit. The three biggest companies were Players cigarettes, Raleigh bicycles and Boots the chemist. Only Boots keeps anything like its former level of activity. The city was also a commercial centre for the coalfields to the north, where the small towns are now heavy with unemployed. The centre of the city still hums with activity, but the postwar council estates are full of jobless young with nothing constructive to do.

The Nottingham Christian Action Network (NCAN) was one of the first to get off the ground, perhaps because Mannie Stewart who first pioneered it had already compiled a Directory and also had the backing of The Christian Centre, Nottingham, his home church, who gave him office space and time to start it up. Mansfield Road Baptist Church also gave time to Anne Davies, one of their associate ministers, and a big

Independent Evangelical Church, Cornerstone, helped financially. Four fifths of the Evangelical churches backed the network.

The projects in the Network include those aimed to train for employment, help children, young mothers, young people, the disabled, ethnic groups, the homeless, prostitutes, those needing rehabilitation from alcoholism and drugs, the lonely, families under strain, individuals in stress and depression, and those suffering from Aids.

The churches appointed a steering group of four, chaired by Anne Davies, who has been a manager in the Social Services and has helped to develop a family centre in her own church.

James Harvey, the treasurer, is a community officer in Macedon, the largest voluntary provider of housing in Nottingham and, though a secular organisation, it has strong support from the churches.

Anne Anderson is the administrator and works two mornings a week for the Network. She is a graduate with a degree in psychology.

Mannie Stewart, undoubtedly the driving force behind the formation of the Network, remains an active member, though he is now development officer for all the networks. This steering group reflects the need we felt at the beginning, to have mainly lay people with some experience in social work, and lots of experience in getting things done! They ask individuals, churches and organisations to subscribe as members of the Network and offer 'founder membership' of the Network for £250 or more.

The Network produces a quarterly newsletter to keep all members, including projects, in touch with each other, reporting what they are all doing and planning. It also advertises the quarterly network lunch, aimed to help them all get to know each other. To help this along they adapt the custom of some hostesses, who make every other person move two to the right at the end of each course.

The Nottingham Council for Voluntary Services is a partner in a couple of initiatives by members of the network. They are heavily funded by the city and many employees of the Council work on secondment to them. So the Network can perhaps build on that relationship.

They have also had a request from the Chief Inspector of Police in one of the crime-ridden suburbs to see whether the Network could talk to the churches about a better use of their youth groups or start new groups or activities. So they have helped steer an initiative to coordinate church youth activity, to swap ideas between those already involved in the area, to raise resources through partnership with the Council for a youth drop-in and in the creation of youth forums to allow the young to have a voice in issues which concern them. We can only hope it works. We once visited another Nottingham suburb where the new youth club, financed by the Church Urban Fund, was surrounded by steel railings, twelve feet high to prevent its being vandalised.

The Network has started a course in basic counselling skills, helped by two highly qualified Christian counsellors and a local Further Education College, who have employed them part-time. They have written and teach a twelve week intensive course designed for people in church projects who will be examined by the City and Guilds board. At the time of writing 56 people had completed the course and another 30 have been enrolled on a new course. They intend to run the course in two other places nearby.

The Network have also taken part in a consultation on homelessness, which made them feel the need for much better relations between the churches and the para-church organisations which are involved in social action. They think the answer may be a small team of consultants, perhaps advised by other Christian agencies who can help church leadership groups develop effective and professional social action.

The London Borough of Hackney

Hackney is not only a poor inner-city borough, it has an exceptionally high population of refugees, including a large number of Turkish Kurds, who have come because there are so many other refugees there already! But new refugees have no English and, if they get into problems with their social service entitlement, have no way of getting answers to their questions. And their temporary legal status makes accommodation difficult. Some may be in hiding because they face deportation and it is difficult for the church to help those whom the state sees as criminals.

Crime and drug abuse are both widespread in Hackney, though concentrated in limited areas. The churches find it hard to deal with them without specialist resources.

The Vicarage of St Luke's in Hackney is a biggish early Victorian house, looking out over a terrace of dowdy but well-preserved eighteenth-century town houses, which would be gentrified if they were anywhere but in Hackney. The Rector, David Hewitt, who chairs the Hackney Network, is one's ideal picture of a Church of England Vicar, kindly, courteous, and enthusiastic, but for all his gentle manner he also has experience, like Bishop David Sheppard, of helping to run an east-end youth club.

Above all, he has a care for all who live in his parish, black, white, or Asian, and the refugees from all around the world. Perhaps because no one race dominates, there is real racial cooperation. In other cities and boroughs the high rate of unemployment and the deprivation which comes with it do not bring people together as they have in Hackney. David Hewitt thinks that the African culture of mutual family obligation also helps to make the difference in Hackney.

Another factor is probably David Hewitt himself. He chaired the Hackney Evangelical Fellowship until it was wound down recently, and he seems to have a way of holding together leaders from all the different denominations that make it up. The Evangelical Fellowship arose out of a forum for unity between black and white-majority evangelical churches. Although most black churches are evangelical, this kind of co-operation should be far more frequent than it is. Another reason for unity may be the small size of most of the churches in Hackney. St Luke's has a congregation of about 100 at the time of writing, and several other churches have around 70, but many are even smaller than that.

From the beginning, the Hackney Evangelical Fellowship was concerned with social needs, so the Network fitted in easily with its objectives. The committee of the Evangelical Fellowship functioned as the steering group of the Network. The chair, David Hewitt, represented the Anglicans and there was one Pentecostal, two Baptists, three from the Black churches and another Anglican who is a youth worker. It appears that in spite of the changes surrounding the Evangelical Fellowship, and David Hewitt's role being taken over by another local church leader, the Network will be able to continue with much active support. The churches of the Fellowship seem to be heavily and actively involved in the projects, many of which have been set up by the churches themselves.

Hackney Employment Link Project (H.E.L.P.) was set up with the help of the PECAN project in Peckham (described above) and is supported by seven churches. It aims, like PECAN, to help prepare people for training and jobs and, also like PECAN, has a 70% success rate. But, though it has had help from the European Social Fund, it ran out of money and had to be disbanded. It had been hoping to get a subsidy as part of the Government's New Deal programme, but the outlook for restarting the project is not good and anything that is revived would have to begin again as a completely new organisation.

The 'Cosmo Club' aims to help children aged 5-12 on the estates. It is run by Hampden Chapel, and is based on a mini-bus, which goes to a different estate each day. It is a focus of attention and they find they can reach far more children by going to them than by persuading them to travel to a youth club. And by travelling around it touches far more children. Its main activity is outdoor games and it gives strong ethical teaching with a Christian basis. Because of its teaching against drugs and vandalism, it is warmly supported by both local police and council. Those who run the club also take about two hundred school assemblies a year and Scripture Union have helped them run a holiday scheme for children and teenagers.

The Meeting Field scheme is a vision of a new community centre run by St Luke's which, when it is completed will have a gym (with special facilities for the disabled) and fitness centre, adult education classes (especially strong on language and literacy) and a homework club. It is being financed initially by the sale of an old and redundant church hall. It could also house a Credit Union, which is a secular project and very necessary in Hackney. The whole scheme is to be run in partnership with Hackney Council. The old church hall has been sold to Providence Row Housing Association who will construct fifteen flats for 'move on' accommodation for people who have been homeless.

Barnados have started Church's Neighbourhood Development in London (CANDL) to help churches on drug education and to help those who have suffered from sexual abuse.

Hackney Evangelical Youth aims to bring church youth group leaders together for mutual support and encouragement. They do make a difference. When we visited one of the most notorious estates in Hackney, the young vicar showed us the centre where they held their youth club and then as we turned into the bleak high-rise flats, a menacing figure came towards us. The vicar said, 'Don't worry, he's one of ours. I baptised him a couple of weeks ago.' The figure in shabby trainers, t-shirt and jeans, flashed a brilliant smile as he passed by.

There are more projects, a shop for second-hand clothing, with counselling laid on, a club for single mothers and a club for the disabled in Hoxton (in better times the birthplace of the Frederick Catherwood, artist and architect and friend of the poet Keats, who was the first to draw the Maya temples in Yucatan). Both of these projects are in St John's Church, which had a lottery grant for the needed refurbishment. And seven churches take it in turn to open one night a week (for the first three months of the year) for those who would otherwise be out on the streets.

We were also very impressed by a club for the elderly run by a black Pentecostal church. The old folk mostly lived on their own and found it hard to get out and the club was the centre of their social life.

On an altogether different scale, Hackney has the old Mildmay Hospital, which has been converted as a hospice for those dying of AIDS. I had not realised all the dire consequences of the collapse of all immune systems until I went round that hospice. It now has a special wing for mothers with AIDS and their babies, who are born HIV positive.

Beyond these projects in which the Fellowship is closely involved, there are other projects which they feel should go in the directory that they hope to publish shortly.

Although it would help Hackney to be in a wider network, including some of the richer boroughs further out, there was a lot of opposition when we suggested this. In London, the borough is the local community and, even in the East End, each borough sees itself as quite different from all its neighbours and with nothing at all in common with those in the faraway leafy suburbs on the outer edge of the great city.

But that strong sense of identity has certainly created a Fellowship and Network in which quite different churches and races work strongly together and, however small their resources, they seem to do great good. It is also a community where the churches and public services work together without fuss and help each other face the awful problems of poverty, unemployment and the insidious drug culture that those problems encourage.

Southampton

Southampton is a city of 213,000 and is still a thriving port, despite the loss of some passenger traffic and the cross-channel ferry. It has less unemployment than cities further north. But it has all the other social problems. There is the same separation of rich and poor, one to the west of the river and the other to the east and most of the 6% who attend church come from the richer western side.

The Southampton network was set up by the Southampton Local Evangelical Fellowship (LEF), which covers nearly half the churches in the city. The LEF set up the Southampton Christian Action Network and its steering group is chaired by a member of the Local Evangelical Fellowship executive. So there is a very strong commitment of the churches to the Network and social action is high on the agenda of the churches.

The Southampton Network is, after the Hackney pattern, limited to a relatively small number of projects in each of which the steering group, currently chaired by Chris Davis, the Director of the City Mission, take an active interest. Two of the projects are run by the City Mission itself. With the smaller number of projects, the Directory give a half-page description of each project showing exactly what it does and the limit of its capacity.

The main projects under the care of the Network are,

Groundswell, which looks after about twenty people suffering from AIDS, many being women who would not otherwise get any help. They could look after more if they had more volunteers.

Door which, like Prison Fellowship supports prisoners and their families and helps through the process of reintegration into society.

Hope (UK) This is the Solent branch of a national drug education organisation and works with schools, youth groups and parent groups. It could also use more volunteers.

The Salvation Army, which runs a residential detox centre for alcoholics.

Nightstop, which finds hosts to put up 18 to 25 year olds for a few nights. It hosts about 400 people a year and has two full-time and one part-time staff. The office is used as a drop-in centre, though the downside is that the staff are vulnerable to verbal abuse and threatening behaviour from those who don't get what they want.

Central Counselling Service is run by the Community Church and linked to the Association of Christian Counsellors.

Basics Bank aims to feed and clothe people on very low incomes who cannot provide for themselves, and also asylum seekers, who are all referred to them by over 100 agencies, including the social services. It feeds or clothes an average of about thirteen people a day and is limited by space and the number of volunteers and donations from food shops.

Dorcas is a furniture re-cycling project run by the City Mission and is limited by space and security – it has suffered from arson attacks.

Safe helps the jobless find work or training courses. It has a staff of eight and about 120 people a year complete the programme and 70% find work or training.

Firgrove, a pregnancy crisis centre (see above).

Gate, a project for prostitutes in the city centre.

The City Mission is acting as the lead organisation for the Network in developing a Credit Union (see the section on debt above). Twenty churches have given their support to the idea and the steering group are looking at the possibility of writing a common bond which would give the criteria for membership.

The Network sees its role as a forum for support of project leaders, to help them find volunteers and funding – they decided that it would be invidious for the Network itself to raise funds and allocate them between different projects. They aim to produce a newsletter four times a year to keep churches and projects in touch and to point out where help is needed.

The public launch of the Southampton Evangelical Association five years ago paved the way for a good relationship with the City Council, and it was after this launch that the Network came into being. Now representatives of the Evangelical Alliance, with 'Churches Together,' which represents many of the other churches, and the City Council meet together regularly as the City Liaison Group. And Chris Davis, as Director of the City Mission and members of other projects meet with the City Council in their own right.

The Council refers a great many people in need to the projects of the Network, and has been able to help to a limited extent with funding. But since it became a regional authority, it, like the local Health Authority, has been chronically short of money.

7

Agenda for the Churches

The Church is not a social club

Having looked at the extent of the social breakdown, we need to look at what the Church and the State should do about it and how they can best work together.

Today's Christian Church finds itself on the margins of British society. It is treated as one religion among many. The State has taken away its long-standing social functions and it has become, for too many of its members, a club for like-minded people. Some find the music and ambience of the Orthodox attractive; others swing with the uninhibited singing of the Charismatics; many hold to the worship of the established Church because of its antiquity and its ritual; some like preachers who make them feel good. But if churches take on the mind-set of the consumer society, seeking maximum personal satisfaction, we deserve to be on the margins.

But that mind-set is not what Christ taught his disciples nor what the Apostles taught the early Church. They taught us that we are here to love God, to love our neighbours and, through that, to change society for the better.

None of the projects we've looked at are on the margins of society. They are all in the thick of it, where the trouble is worst and are dealing with problems that the world prefers to ignore. Paul told the Corinthian church, which preferred preachers trained in rhetoric to his own plain teaching (I Cor. 4.20), 'The kingdom of God is not a matter of talk but of power.'

Christ gave the Church the public duty to be the 'salt of the earth' and the 'light of the world.' If we are only a social club, if, as Christ warned in the Sermon on the Mount (Matthew 5, 13) the salt has lost its saltiness, 'then it is no longer good for anything but to be thrown out and trampled by men.'

The ingredient which gives the Christian that essential salty tang and which brings them to the heart of most social problems is love. It is the same love which brought Christ to a stable in Bethlehem and then to his death on a wooden cross. The Church is here to serve our community, as Christ served his and earns its right to be heard by showing love, as Christ did, in a selfish and cynical world.

The experience of all the projects we have looked at runs true to the same form. What they did for those in need came first. Only then and often 'only if they asked' would they add the reasons for their Christian faith. A world that knows less and less about unselfish love needs, not just words, but the example of love to convey the message of a God of love. That is the source of the Church's power.

'Who is my neighbour?'

Christ did not leave any doubt about the extent of our duty. An 'expert on the law,' who had replied correctly that the second great commandment was to love ones neighbour as oneself, asked 'Who is my neighbour?' Clearly he did not want the list of neighbours to be too long. One must draw the line somewhere.

But Christ answered with the famous parable of the Good Samaritan, who helped the man lying robbed and half dead on the Jericho road, after a Priest and a Levite had passed by on the other side. Jesus asked (Luke 10), 'Which of these was neighbour to the man who fell into the hands of the robbers?' The lawyer answered, 'The one who had mercy on him' and Jesus told him, 'Go and do likewise.'

The rub of the story is that the Jews were not on speaking terms with their Samaritan neighbours, whose mixed-race forebears had settled in the land and whose religion was a bastard mix of Jewish and local religions.

Yet a Samaritan was the hero of the story, the true neighbour showing the love the Jews professed, but which the two Jewish religious leaders had not practised. So Christian love must be extended beyond those who are members of our own church and raceto all who need our help. That includes all the needy in our own city, whether fellow citizens or strangers.

Christ himself practised what he preached. He healed the sick, because God is love and his heart went out to them, although he knew that most of those whom he helped would turn away from his teaching.

In Mark's account of the feeding of the five thousand (Mark 6), the disciples said to Jesus when he had finished teaching the crowd,

> Send the people away, so that they can go to the surrounding countryside and find themselves something to eat.

But he refused and on the later very similar occasion, (Mark 8), he gives his reasons,

> I have compassion on these people because they have already been with me three days and have nothing to eat. If I send them home hungry, they will collapse on the way, because they have come a long distance.

His teaching, what he called 'food for the soul,' mattered. But we are body as well as soul and Christ cares for the whole person. God made both body and soul and Christ cares for both. Who are his followers to care less than he does?

The Apostle Paul had the same care for his rough, brutal and selfish fellow travellers on his last recorded voyage (Acts 27). Having used his right as a Roman citizen to appeal to Caesar against the false accusations of the Jewish leaders, he found himself a prisoner in a ship bound for Rome. With him were other prisoners, brutal soldiers and selfish sailors, and the ship was in the hands of a careless captain – as unloveable a bunch of characters as anyone could find. But Paul did not retreat into a holy huddle with his friend Luke. He cared for his hard-bitten shipmates.

He knew his native coast well and warned that it was too late in the season to set sail from Crete. His advice was ignored and when the storm blew up it was so bad and so prolonged that the crew gave up hope. So he prayed to God for the safety of the ship's company and, next morning, told them that God had answered his prayer and that, though the ship would be wrecked, all the company would be saved.

The crew were encouraged and went back to their posts. Their soundings told them that they were near land, but they decided that this was the moment to make off in the long-boat and leave the rest to their fate. It was only the ever-watchful Paul who was alert enough to spot what they were up to. He told the Centurion, who ordered the soldiers to cut off the long-boat to keep the crew on board.

Then, ever caring and ever practical, Paul told them that unless they all had something to eat, they would not have the strength to get to shore. When finally, they had all got through the surf, some swimming and some on bits of timber from the wreck, our last picture of the great Apostle is of his gathering sticks for a fire to dry them all out. The love of Christ cannot be divided into compartments, it must permeate the whole of life.

The teaching of Christ and the Apostles is that words are meaningless without deeds. In his defence before King Agrippa (Acts 26), Paul says,

> I preached that they should repent and turn to God and prove their repentance by their deeds.

James spells this out (James 2)

> What good is it my brothers if a man claims to have faith, but has no deeds? Can such faith save him? Suppose a brother or sister is without clothes and daily food. If one of you says to him, 'Go, I wish you well; keep warm and well fed.' but does nothing about his physical needs, what good is it? In the same way, faith by itself, if it is not accompanied by action, is dead.

Not only is Christian teaching clear, but when, in the end, Christ as Judge separates the sheep from the goats, he does it by proof of our deeds. Christ said, (Matthew 25),

> The King will say to those who are blessed, 'I was hungry, but you

gave me something to eat, I was thirsty and you gave me something to drink, I was a stranger and you invited me in, I needed clothes and you clothed me, I was sick and you looked after me, I was in prison and you came to visit me. . . . Whatever you did for one of the least of these my brothers, you did for me.'

To the others, who also professed to be his followers, but did not do any of these things, he says,

"Whatever you did not do for the least of these, you did not do for me" and, despite their professions of faith, they are excluded from his eternal kingdom.

How the Christian Church earned its influence

The long history of the Church is a story of the power of Christian love and the huge influence in society which came from that power.

There is little doubt that it was this neighbourly love that made it so hard for the Roman Emperors to wipe out the Christian Church by persecution. Christians were good, reliable and loving neighbours, obedient and productive citizens and one persecution after another faded out as the Church's reputation grew until, in 313, the Emperor Constantine's Edict of Milan marked his own support of the Christian faith.

The great Roman Empire had less than two centuries left, but the Christian faith was not dependent on Roman rule. Richard Fletcher's magisterial book, *The Conversion of Europe* records the way in which the faith spread after the fall of the Empire. The Burgundians, Ostrogoths and Vandals were the first pagan tribes to be converted to the Christian faith. But they had all been near to Roman civilisation and, when they took over, they seem to have adopted the Roman customs, including its religion.

But the fifth-century pagan invaders had no similar respect. In looking at later stories of conversion Fletcher says,

Royal hesitation is a notable feature of our narratives. Clovis, Ethelbert and Edwin all took their time. Abandonment of the old gods was no light matter. Consultation with counsellors was prudent. How would the pagan priesthood react? There are difficult questions here about the dynamics of a king's authority over his kinsfolk, his realm and his vassal kingdoms. Giving a lead did not always work, even within the Royal family.

So how did Christians succeed in hostile pagan territory? The answer seems to be that, as with the early Church, love was more powerful than the sword. The early monasteries were simple mission stations where the Christians taught the local children, looked after the sick, took in the traveller and led self-sacrificing and loving lives which stood in sharp contrast to the selfish lives of those around them. Because most of the mission stations, such as Fulda deep in the German forests, had become rich monasteries half a millennium later, we forget their simple beginnings. But it was those beginnings which were critical to the acceptance of Christianity right across Europe.

In our own islands, Patrick went from Wales, the only unconquered part of Roman Britain, to convert the Irish as 'a slave in Christ to a foreign people.' (p 86) and he encouraged the monastic way of life. Columba went from Ireland to the tiny mission station of Iona to convert the Scots. The Scottish Christians came south to Lindisfarne in Northern England, then to Jarrow and Whitby as the Christian missionaries to Kent came north to meet them. Nothing less than their simple self-sacrifice would have converted the brutal pagan tribes.

There was a united church in England before there was a united kingdom of England. Its moral authority, from the ninth century on, had been earned. As we enter the third millennium, we should never forget the great achievements of the Church in the first millennium.

In the early part of the second millennium, Europe became more settled and the Church became rich and powerful. Kings, worried about that power, began to appoint their own placemen as Archbishops and Bishops. Sometimes the new Archbishop refused to play. King Henry II made one of his own men Archbishop of Canterbury, but Thomas Becket unexpectedly took the Church's side and was murdered by the King's knights. By the fourteenth century, Chaucer had little good to say about the clerics on pilgrimage to the martyr's tomb, except for the poor Lollard parson who really cared for his flock.

The sixteenth-century Reformation led to a more austere Church, with the Jesuits setting the pace on the Catholic side and the Puritans on the Protestant. But the princes still fought on in the sixteenth and seventeenth centuries to keep their patronage and power over the Church. This died hard in southern and eastern Europe, but in northern Europe it was broken by emigration to North America, by the French revolution of 1789 and both the United States and France became secular states.

In Britain it was broken by legal toleration of dissenters and the rise in the eighteenth century of the Methodist movement. With the arrival of the Methodists the influence of the whole Church was once more dependent on its evident care for all around it. In the eigtheenth and nineteenth centuries, the greatest Christian leaders were in the forefront of the care for the needs of the ordinary people. Whitfield crossed and recrossed the Atlantic to raise money for the orphanage he had set up in Georgia. Side by side with John Wesley's teaching went organisation of the Methodist Societies to help those in need.

At the end of the eighteenth century lay leaders in the Church of England, known as the Clapham Sect and inspired by William Wilberforce led the campaign which succeeded in abolishing the slave trade between Africa and America. In the next generation, Lord Ashley (later Earl of Shaftesbury) spent the whole of his long life fighting for the underdog, especially those who were being exploited by the owners of the new factories, which were springing up all over the country. He was also the first to see that the mentally ill were properly housed and cared for. Elizabeth Fry led prison reform and Florence Nightingale the reform of nursing and hospitals.

At the end of the nineteenth century, the great upsurge in the Christian faith and the energetic drive for social care both died down. Though the streets of London were packed for the funeral of Lord Shaftesbury in 1885, no one took on his political leadership. Charles Spurgeon, the greatest nineteenth-century preacher left an orphanage near the Metropolitan Tabernacle, but no one took his place of leadership when he died in 1892.

Twentieth-century nationalism and materialism

The new religion of the twentieth century was nationalism. The flag took the place of the cross and in 1914 the armies of Europe marched out, each under its own flag, to a slaughter of 15 million, only surpassed by the 35 million killed in World War II. Two decades after that war, secular humanism took the place of the Church as moral arbiter.

Today, another thirty years on, the policies of unfettered markets have unleashed forces of unfettered greed and the removal of the belief in Christ as the Son of God has produced the greatest increase in superstition and paganism since the dark ages. People guide their lives by the horoscopes in the popular press, every superstition banned by Moses three thousand years ago is alive and flourishing in Britain today and the pagan rites that go with them are creeping back too.

The secular humanists seem to believe that it is in the interests of human freedom that we should all believe what we want and do what we like. Since that is no response to the social problems, they are forced on the one hand to deny the problems and on the other to invent their own set of rules of 'political correctness.'

The argument for freedom of thought and speech is one which the Church worldwide supports. But each individual right of action depends on a corresponding duty by others to respect that right and it is those duties that pose the problem for the humanists. Theirs is not an organised popular movement, experienced in persuading wide classes of people on their duties in daily life. It is easy to get a hearing for the removal of restraints, but to gain wide voluntary acceptance of a structure of individual duties to make those rights effective is beyond their reach.

So secular humanists demand that the State delivers a legal order on which they can rely. By contrast, the Church aims to deliver a moral order on which the State can rely. This is why the Church can be infinitely stronger as a partner for the State. But today we have to show, as never before, that we can deliver a better moral order, based on everyone's care for their neighbours.

The need, once more, to win hearts and minds

So there is a huge responsibility on the Church to win hearts and minds for a Christian moral order on which a new, fairer and more benign social order can be based. Our brief excursion through the history of the Church shows that this is best done from the bottom up by the behaviour and actions of ordinary Christians. Wilberforce, Shaftesbury and others may have led the reforms of their day, but it was the widespread national support that drove them through.

It is, in the end, love and not argument which melts the human heart and, as the stories above show, that love is needed as never before in our country. The Christian's duty to love our neighbour, is quite clear, but duty is not a popular word, even among professing Christians, and people give all kinds of reasons for not following it.

Three weak excuses

The first excuse is that the poor are government's responsibility and the more Christians are willing to help them, the more the government will shuffle off to the Church.

No doubt it was the Roman army's duty to patrol the Jericho road and to keep it free from robbers. Some such argument may have flitted through the minds of the Priest and the Levite as they passed the wounded man on the other side of the road. But the simple kindness of the Samaritan told him otherwise. There was no time to blame someone else. The man would die unless he was helped at once.

In any case the mood of our country is now so materialistic that government, which mirrors those who put it there, believes that it cannot raise the taxes to fund the welfare State. Government is not entirely cynical, but it judges that far the most sensitive issue in public policy is the level of taxation and the more the churches do on our own, the more we are entitled to argue the case for government help.

When the causes of the social problems are debated, government will listen to those who are in the front line, who are doing their best to help and who know what they are talking about. The strength of the Church is that it is in every ward in every parliamentary constituency, so we should concentrate on the grass roots, where our strengths are. On the last count, active church membership was 6.4 million. Secular humanism cannot match that in either organised numbers or in coverage.

The second common argument is that the Church's priority is to preach the gospel and that social work is a distraction; it is only for this short life and saving of souls is for eternity. And only if people become Christians will they get their lives in order and be able to get on top of their problems.

This was not, however, Jesus' way. He both healed and preached, even though he knew that many would not listen to the teaching, because love is indivisible and unconditional. And how can we persuade people of a God of love, who gave his Son to die for their sins, if we do not show that loving care ourselves in a way that they can understand? If we care for the material needs which people feel most acutely, they are, at very least, more likely to listen to us if we tell them of a spiritual need which they have not yet felt.

The argument also ignores the division of effort between preacher and congregation. The duty of the minister to preach does not prevent members of the congregation from doing their duty to their neighbours. In one traditional inner-city church that argued the priority of the gospel, I asked how many strangers came to listen to it and it was clear from their embarrassment that the answer was none. By contrast, a nearby church, which had a very active social work, was filled with new Christians.

The third argument is that this is the 'social gospel' and we are meant to preach the gospel of salvation. In the early twentieth century, many churches no longer preached the personal and unpopular message of sin and salvation, but concentrated instead on 'social sins' to be dealt with by political action. This shift of responsibility on to government was no more appreciated by politicians than it was by the traditional churches.

No one was stronger in his denunciations of the 'social gospel' than my late father-in-law, Dr Martyn Lloyd-Jones, when Minister of Westminster Chapel and his name is often used by those who argue against social action. But he had nothing whatever against the Church helping those in need. The Clapham youth club referred to above, was actively supported by both Westminster Chapel and its Minister.

To quote from a book of his sermons on the Acts, he said that the 'social gospel' was about 'the state of society and the affairs of the nation. So they put aside the old gospel and . . . taught the people to stop attending places of worship; they said that all this could be done through politics. By passing acts of Parliament you could get a perfect world.'

It is quite clear that the 'social gospel' he attacks is not the work of churches in feeding the hungry and housing the homeless, which is at the heart of this book. The failed effort of the 'social gospel' is much nearer to the position of today's secular humanists.

Church and State

Christians living in a democracy, will want to influence government policy just as much as any other citizen. The question is how we do this, and that depends on the right and proper relationship between State and Church.

The Jewish leaders asked Jesus whether it was right to give tribute to Caesar or not. They hoped that he would be in trouble with Jewish nationalist feeling if he said yes and with the Romans if he said no. His answer was neither yes nor no, that both State and Church had a legitimate call on our loyalty. He said, 'Give to Caesar the things that are Caesars and to God the things that are God's.' Both Church and State need our support.

The Apostle Paul spelt this out in his letter to the Romans (Chapter 13).

> The authorities which exist have been established by God. He is God's servant to do you good. But if you do wrong, do not be afraid, for he does not bear the sword for nothing. . . . This is also why you pay taxes, for the authorities are God's servants, who give their whole time to governing. If you owe taxes, pay taxes . . . if respect, then respect, if honour, then honour.

The Apostle Peter in his first letter says (Chapter 2),

> Submit yourself, for the Lord's sake, to every authority instituted among men, to the king . . . or to governors who are sent by him to punish those who do wrong and to commend those who do right.

So the State as well as the Church is ordained of God and the Church must not get above itself and try to take the political power which God has given to governments. But in democracies, each citizen has an individual responsibility as a citizen in choosing the government. And since governments are put over us, in Peter's words, 'to punish those who do wrong and to commend those who do right,' the government has to make moral decisions. It cannot act in a moral vacuum.

The prophetic role of the Church

The Church has a matching public moral role, the same role of moral guardian as was exercised by the Old Testament prophets, the same duty to set the bad behaviour of rulers against the laws of duty and justice to the widows, orphans, aliens and the poor, all made in the image of God the Creator.

Isaiah (5,8) condemns those who have expropriated the land and means of livelihood of fellow citizens and pronounces

> Woe to you who add house to house and field to field until no space is left and you live alone in the land.

The prophets warned with growing urgency of what would happen if God's law was ignored. They said that Israel would go into captivity and that Jerusalem would be destroyed. Moral delinquency brought catastrophe then and is just as likely to do so today. The Apostle John saw the destruction of a new Babylon through the eyes of merchants and sea captains who said, 'In one hour she has been brought to ruin.' (Revelation 18).

Once it allows itself to become subservient to the State, the Church's prophetic role is extinguished. That is why, in the sixteenth and seventeenth centuries, the State was so unwilling to let go. The Monarch appointed the Bishops and, as James I so famously said, 'No bishop, no king.' State and Church should work in **equal** partnership, each doing its own job for the good of the nation.

The Law and the Prophets of the Old Testament give role models of social responsibility which are still valid today. The drastic penalties of martial law, needed for an armed people on the march between ruthless enemies, are no longer valid. The ceremonial laws have been overtaken by Christ's sacrifice, once for all, for the sins of those who trust him.

But the civil laws of Moses, which look forward to their future settlement in Caanan, are shot through with the duty of care for our neighbours and their belongings. The ten commandments have lost nothing of their validity and the family, including the enlarged family, is central to the social structure. If we think that that was all a long time ago, we should note that there has been no new sin in three thousand years and that all the sins in the time of Moses are still with us today.

Today no nation can claim to be God's special people, but the prophetic ministry was not confined to Israel alone. The prophets denounced the sins of all the surrounding nations. God sent Jonah to Nineveh to warn of their destruction unless they repented. That upset Jonah, who hadn't wanted to go in the first place and now was appalled that a repentant Nineveh had earned a reprieve. But God told him, 'Nineveh has more than a hundred and twenty thousand people, should not I be concerned about that great city?'

In any case, Britain not only has a long history of Christian faith, but so much that has shaped our country comes from our Christian heritage, the scientific method, democracy and the rule of law, business integrity, the professional duty of care and, famously, our sense of fair play. We should know better than to poison our own roots.

So it must be open to the Church to act as moral mentor to the State on what is wrong and what is right. Beyond that it should be open to the State to make a judgement on what wrongs are private and must be left to God to judge and what should be subject to legal restraint.

The moral basis of the social order

Christians are especially justified in opposing the current deconstruction of a Christian moral order, which has developed slowly, by trial and error, over thirteen centuries. That long process of curbing evil and encouraging good is at least open and on the record. We can see where and why it has succeeded and where and why, for a time, it failed. But the short thirty years of deconstruction of the moral and social order has shown nothing but catastrophic failure. Yet despite the strength of its case, the Church needs to be wise in the way it puts its arguments.

It will not win the war on single issues. That does not mean that it should give up citadels without a fight. 'Keep Sunday special' put up a brilliant fight. One day a week when most activities close down, puts a rhythm of rest in place of unremitting work and protects our health and sanity. It is also absurdly uneconomic to increase costs by a sixth (or a third if they pay double time on Sunday as they should) for no extra sales. That is why so many shops, as well as the trades unions, were against it. But Sunday trading was the flagship for the new materialism and there is a limit to what voluntary bodies can do against the resources of the State.

So the Church will not succeed until it deals with the main issue, which is the moral basis on which our social order should be founded. And in this fight it has to choose ground on which it is strong and the deconstructionists weak.

Church and State at the grass-roots

Secular humanism is strongest in the national media, in films, pop music, theatre and literature. It is weakest at the grass roots, where the Church is strongest. Humanists are strong in the think-tanks, on which government relies so heavily for input to policy. They are weak in their ability to deliver public consent to policies of political correctness that would aim to stop the rot and recover a healthy society. Given all the weakness of human nature, the corruption of established order is far easier than the long hard slog of putting it back together again. But, before it is too late, government must find ways to recover a healthy society.

The huge merit of democracy is that, in the end, government rests on the consent of elected representatives and not on intellectuals in think-tanks. I spent fifteen years as an elected representative and what mattered to me was what mattered to the people I represented. Letters from other constituencies were swiftly passed on to colleagues who represented them, letters from national lobbies went to colleagues who were dealing with the issue and circulars were binned at once. But every single letter from my own patch, was read, considered, worked on – passed to ministers or commissioners if need be – and the final answer topped and tailed in my own hand.

MPs sitting in Westminster may not yet be too worried by fears that the whole country is going downhill. The urgent day to day issues drive out the most important. But talk to them about the awful problems in their own patch and that is a different matter. In the stories above, two Bristol MPs worry about the loan sharks in Bristol, two Sheffield MPs worry about the unemployed in Sheffield. MPs listen to the views of those dealing with the problems on what has caused them. The broader the local group which gives advice about the causes of the problems, the more they are likely to accept them.

Policies do change with a growing consensus in the House of Commons. Put a proposal to a Home Secretary or any cabinet minister and their first calculation is not the theoretical merits of the case, but whether it could get through the House of Commons. Even with the Poll Tax, the Commons view prevailed in the end. Any major change in government policy has to be broadly and deeply based.

That is why I believe that any major effort to change policy should start with discussions between the churches and the local councillors and MPs. Partnership between State and Church does not need to be confined to Westminster and Lambeth. National discussions should be the end of the process and not the beginning.

There is also the problem of Church protocol, who exactly talks to whom, at national level. And when they do talk, the stakes are higher, the debates more tense, government less certain whether those to whom they are talking are really representative or not, least of all whether they could do anything substantive to help.

The local politicians are much clearer about who is genuinely trying to help and who is not. Engaged and committed churches create a group with a common experience and common aim. Since the view of one single city is only a stage in the national debate, the discussions can be more open and the options more frankly discussed. And, since conclusions are likely to differ from one city to another, the views which finally reach government will provide a wider range of options.

So starting at local level would be a sound first step towards a constructive partnership between Church and State.

8

Agenda for Government

Since secular humanism took over the role of moral mentor from the Christian church, the effect, on any reckoning, has been moral chaos and social disaster.

We've looked at a cross-section of that disaster and its effect on individuals. Just a glance at the national figures shows how widespread it is.

Although sheer common sense calls for the use of all our available human resources, the long postwar policy of full employment has been abandoned and unemployment has varied between at least a million and a half in good times and well over three million in bad times. The cost of paying people to do nothing plus the loss of tax revenue is, as we reckoned above, well over £25bn a year.

The switch from direct progressive taxes to taxes on everyone's consumption takes 50% more from the income of the poor than from the rich. So the increase in national wealth has gone to those who need it least, the rich have got very much richer, the poor have got poorer and beggars have reappeared on the streets.

Along with the increases in unemployment and poverty, the latest (1999) edition of *Social Trends* shows that prison population has risen by 50% and is at an all-time high, and that and drug abuse has increased dramatically. The number of registered drug addicts has doubled in five years and police seizures of heroin have trebled. Lone parent families have gone up, as we have seen, from 7% in 1972 to 21% in 1998, most of them mothers.

The legislation introduced in the 1960s to enable doctors to protect the health of the pregnant mother has turned into abortion on demand and the deaths of unborn children, running at about 170,000 a year, have wiped out a large part of the generation on whose income their parents will depend for their pensions. This will fall especially hard on those who rely on state pensions and government has now started to wonder what they can do about it.

The question we began to ask in the last chapter was what a renewed partnership between Church and State could do to put right what has gone wrong.

In all the projects in this book, an unacknowledged, pragmatic partnership was, in fact, at work. In many cases, such as the housing of newly released prisoners, the state simply provided the funding. In others, such as drug rehabilitation, the addicts had to find something to fill the aching gap left by drugs and the moral input of the church-based projects was much more important. In all cases the church-based projects provided the volunteers to help out a hard-pressed state sector, especially the probation service and the social services. When the underlying problem was moral, the church projects were freer to respond. So, as they work together, each finds itself doing what comes naturally.

That may be enough to patch and mend, but if we are to deal with the big issues, there has to be a far wider recognition in the church of its role in underpinning the social order and by the state of the issues which cannot be left to the voluntary sector, but which government alone can deal with. In a survey in 1997 of seventy voluntary social projects, the Evangelical Alliance asked what the projects considered to be the underlying causes of problems with which they were dealing. The two primary causes which came away top of the list were unemployment and the breakup of the family. The church clearly has to take the lead in dealing with the breakup of the family and the state in dealing with unemployment.

Full employment

The church's contribution is to argue in public the moral case for full employment. Christians believe that men and women were made in the image of God the Creator and with the same creative instincts. It is not in our nature to sit about doing nothing; we want to make a contribution which matters to those around us. It is a damaging blow to human dignity to be told that no one wants us. In one project after another we were told that the main problem with the those without work was their feeling of low self worth. It made them much more careless, for instance about becoming addicted to drugs, for what did it matter?

But only government has the economic levers to get the unemployed back to work. The economic case for full employment is the simple one that we will all be better off. Added to that is the political case that it is dangerous to alienate millions of able-bodied citizens. It is especially dangerous to have large numbers of young people in the heart of our major cities with nothing to do and all day to get into trouble; or to take to drugs to block out the misery, and then, once addicted, to begin to commit crimes to finance the habit.

The government's current response is the policies of 'Welfare to Work' and the 'New Deal.' But neither creates higher demand in the labour market and the response of the young is that, without any new jobs at the end, training is just meaningless recycling. So both policies depend too heavily on the threat to remove benefits. But cuts in benefit without more jobs will only squeeze the single mother and the young unemployed even harder.

Before 1979 full employment policies were central to economic policy. Government gave high priority to the achievement of export led growth to produce a foreign trade surplus, maintain employment and fund the welfare state. The trade surplus depended on the ability of British industry to compete with the world's main industrial countries both in their markets, third markets, and in our own home market. Ability to compete depended not just on the cost of labour, but on maintaining the same rate of innovative investment as the rest of Europe, North America and Japan. Despite all the disinformation since then, it was extremely successful. In only three of the last twenty years have we matched the earlier levels of investment and never have we regained anything like the level of employment.

In the twenty years since then, the guiding light of full employment has been abandoned. It was argued that full employment gave too much power to the trades unions, who demanded high progressive taxation in return for wage restraint. What we were given instead was a free for all. Wage restraint was abandoned, taxation on incomes reduced, the resultant trade deficit was financed by borrowing from our main competitors at high rates of interest.

The lower taxes on income were financed by much higher VAT, by the North Sea oil bonanza and then by the sale of public assets. The economy, which used to be regulated by both changes in the level of interest rates and taxes, was regulated by interest rates alone – the essence of the new 'monetarism.' Income tax was put on a downward ratchet. This policy, which its opponents dubbed 'one-handed golf,' put huge strains on interest rates, which were and are, on average, half as high again as those of our main industrial competitors.

The immediate effect of monetarism was to shut down a sixth of British manufacturing industry with the loss of two million jobs. It was only with hard work that the total was not higher. As a director of Goodyear UK, I had to fly to Akron, Ohio, to persuade the main board not to close their biggest UK plant – Wolverhampton's largest industrial employer. Britain's foreign trade surplus survived for a few years on North Sea oil and then plunged deep into the red, where it has remained ever since. Investment for export was not helped by a wildly fluctuating pound and when it was eventually fixed to the European Monetary System, it was at a high exchange rate that was not agreed with our partners and, without their support, could not be sustained. Hence Black Wednesday.

Until after the 1992 election, the policy of the Labour Party had been to end the monetarist experiment. In that election, as mentioned above, John Smith, the shadow chancellor, refused to rule out an increase in taxation. Labour decided that that had lost them the election, changed their policy and, after promises not to raise the rate of income tax for two years, came back to power in 1997.

The reason for this paralysis of government is that secular humanism has made the voters more materialistic. If people are told that this is the only life that there is, then they are tempted to grab what they can, while they can, however they can and to hold on to it hard. Greed is not confined to the rich. Governments reckon that it is the majority who are in work and earning who are the key to any election and that they can ignore the out of work minority. But democracy is government by the majority with the consent of the minority and, if the majority neglects their interests, then, as we have seen in Northern Ireland, the consent of the minority cannot be taken for granted. It is not right morally or safe politically to ride roughshod over minorities. Monetarism ignores this rule; it is a political cover for letting money talk and marginalising those without it.

The monetarists say that we cannot go back to the policies which produced the 'winter of discontent' in 1978-79 and which, they say, allowed the trades unions to hold the country to ransom. I was heavily involved with both management and trades unions in the last two decades of full employment and have walked round more shop floors than most people. The problem was not in the power of the trades unions, but on the shop-floors where a few militants could hold production lines to ransom against the decisions of their union leaders. The majority of employers could buy them off for a fraction of the cost of the stoppage, which they did with great regularity. As the Chairman of one major motor manufacturer told me, 'We are in the business of making cars, not controlling inflation.' As a result those with shop-floor power gained at the expense of those without, the public sector and service industries.

But those days are long past. Employers have rearranged production so that they can no longer be held to ransom and the balance of power in industry has now shifted decisively against the shop floor. The most dramatic shift was when newspapers simply dispensed with all their printers and went over to new technology. The shipping industry dispensed with the dockers and went over to containers, which are now loaded and unloaded away from the port.

Government decided it would not be held to ransom by miners and we now use North Sea oil and gas and cheap imported coal. Manufacturing production lines have been automated, bought out supplies are multi-sourced and trades union membership has dropped steeply. Companies are down-sizing and asking the remaining staff to work harder to make up. If we have a problem today, it is overwork, as the new Scrooges begin to feel their power.

The main problem of paying our way in a fiercely competitive world is that the high interest rates which go with monetarism have kept the pound artificially high and made British industry uncompetitive. Not only does a high pound make our exports more expensive and imports cheaper, but industry is now much more capital-intensive (including money spent on research and development as well as on plant) and interest rates running 50% higher than those of our competitors add hugely and separately to the final costs of new products.

The other cause of high interest rates is the risk of holding a volatile pound. In the last few years the pound has moved from 2.20 to the Deutsche Mark up to 3.10, down again to 2.65 and back to 3.05 at the time of writing. The cost of currency risk alone makes British industry less competitive than French, Dutch or German industries. Boards looking at proposals for investment for export have to allow a big extra risk margin for currency fluctuation and the need for that margin cuts heavily into any investment programme.

So any government which aims to get people back to work has to face up to the disastrous failure of monetarism.

There are two possible ways out. One is a marginal adjustment to the balance between direct and indirect taxation, raising direct taxes and lowering indirect, so that the level of taxes like VAT can be adjusted to curb the economy or to encourage growth. That would take the pressure off interest rates and should allow them to come down to a competitive level, encouraging new job-creating investment. That means some temporary increase in direct taxation until extra tax income from higher growth allows them to drop it back. The government would have to make a case for it as part of the package needed for a return to full employment, with a huge saving in welfare expenditure from the rise numbers at work.

The less paintful way to reduce interest rates and make the pound more competitive is to come to agreement with our European partners on the exchange rate at which they would be prepared to support the pound's return to the European Monetary System.

Since the government wants to make preparations which would enable it to join the Euro after a referendum in 2002 and since a prior period of two years in the EMS is a condition for joining, this seems to be a necessary part of our existing policy. Our partners want us in the Euro and would be reluctant to defend too high a rate for the pound, so they are likely to agree on a much more competitive rate than we have at the time of writing. This would give a substantial one-off boost, through higher exports, to our whole economy.

Against those huge benefits stands false the argument about loss of sovereignty. If the British government really has sovereignty over the rate of the pound, then it is responsible for the loss of half its value between 1979 and 1990. Clearly it had no sovereign power and was not responsible. The pound when the Queen came to the throne in 1952 is now only worth 7p. Were I the Queen, I should order my head to be removed from this devalued currency. When I went into public service in 1964 the pound was said to be in the power of the 'gnomes of Zurich' and shortly before I retired thirty years later, they had been replaced by a Hungarian-born American financier, Mr George Soros.

The argument about sovereignty is no more than a last ditch defence of the failed policy of monetarism. A stable currency and much lower interest rates requires that the decision on interest rates is taken collectively by all the central bankers in the European Monetary Union and we will once more have to lower and raise national taxes (or expenditure) for our own fine tuning. The real issue is about once more accepting that responsibility.

There is another argument used in defence of Anglo-American monetarism. It is that the continental European rate of unemployment is much higher than it is in the UK or the USA. That has several temporary causes which have nothing to do with the 'benefits' of monetarism.

One is that most Community countries depressed their economies in the run up to the 1999 introduction of the Euro, to bring their borrowing under control to meet the conditions of Monetary Union. That is a one-off problem and would not affect us, since we are within the Euro borrowing conditions, even though we have a foreign trade deficit.

Another is that the criticism ignores the huge structural problem of East German unemployment created on the German union by the overvaluation of the East German currency, which priced the unskilled East Germans out of jobs.

The third is that in some major continental countries employers have to add 50% or more on to their wage bill in order to pay for health insurance and pensions, which other countries carry on general taxation. That is no way to maintain full employment, as they now see, and they want to change the system as soon as they can.

Unless the 'Welfare to Work' and the 'New Deal' deliver the trained and eager employees which industry wants to take on, government would be well advised to prepare for expansion by projects for getting young people into real jobs, like those in Derry and Sheffield or, on a larger scale, a scheme like Roosevelt's Conservation Corps. An expanding economy will need more employable workers and government should make sure that we have them.

The breakup of the family

The second huge problem today is the breakup of the family. It is argued that this is a purely personal matter and nothing to do with the government. But, as we've seen, the results of family breakdown impact on the whole of society and bring enormous costs, costs of supporting hundreds of thousands of single mothers, because the father has walked out. There is also a heavy cost to society. If more teenagers drop out of school because one parent alone is not enough to act as a role model and mentor, then we have fewer people capable of working for a living and more on costly benefit; or, worse, we have to have a much heavier and costlier police presence to try to keep order and a huge and expensive increase in the prison population of those who are caught.

It has been the job of the family through the ages, all round the world and in every society and under every religion, to teach children how to live with each other and with those around them. There they are taught that there are sanctions against bad behaviour and rewards for good behaviour. Ideally this should be done against a background of natural love and affection, so that the sanction of disapproval alone is enough. But, one way or the other, the family is the place to learn that selfishness does not pay.

Common sense and experience teach that discipline is far easier if there are two parents to support each other and far more difficult if there is only one. And if children do not learn discipline, it is small wonder that, in so many city estates, law and order have broken down, that the police cannot make the streets and walkways safe for the old and cannot guard the children against the dealers in drugs.

The ability to preserve law and order is the ultimate test of the state, especially of the democratic state, which relies so heavily on the self-discipline and consent of the citizen. Democracy and the rule of law go together. When the rule of law breaks down, people take the law into their own hands; the rich and powerful have security guards and everyone else is on their own. It is an eccentricity of the present political class in the Western world to believe that the family is a purely private affair.

The Christian view of the family

The false prophets of the twentieth century have lampooned the family as a tyrannical institution, from which we all need to be set free. Other faiths can speak for themselves, but the Christian teaching is totally against tyranny in the family. It is that, on the contrary, the obligations within the family are mutual and that all members have obligations to each other.

The Apostle Paul tells the Ephesians (Chapter 5)

> Husbands love your wives as Christ loved the church and gave himself for her. . . . In the same way husbands ought to love their wives as they love their own bodies . . . each one of you must love his wife as he loves himself and the wife must respect her husband.

On the relations between parents and children, Paul says (Chapter 6)

> Honour your father and mother, which is the first commandment
> (of the Ten Commandments) with promise ('that it may go well
> with you'). . . . Fathers do not exasperate your children.

What shines through is this mutuality of obligation. When we asked a young Albanian woman how, in a country where religion had been outlawed for forty years, she had become a Christian, she said that it was the mutual obligation in these passages which first attracted her. 'I said to myself, "That's right, that's what it should be."

In this imperfect world, families are, of course, not perfect. Thousands of novels have been written about heroines whose true love is frustrated by the selfishness or snobbishness of parents. We all know couples who have married in haste and repented at leisure and the world has its share of unhappy families. But today the world is at least as full of the traumatised remnants of failed partnerships.

Couples who both regard marriage as permanent are more careful in entering into its commitments. And, once married, they are more careful to find ways of accommodating one another. Above all, they are more secure in their relationship with each other and that mutual support and security are great prizes, especially for a wife and most especially for the children.

By contrast, uncommitted and experimental partnership is inherently insecure and the insecurity in the relationship is likely to increase anxiety, suspicion and distrust, so it is not surprising that these partnerships are more fragile and break up far more easily and, if the partners themselves escape unscarred, the children certainly do not. One daughter of a broken marriage said simply, 'There can be nothing worse in childhood than losing one of your parents.'

The least the government can do is to recognise the support for the family of all organised religions in Britain and it might then go on to consider its own interest in the stability of the family. Then, just as government are quick to recognise the financial implications of any proposals which come to it, so it should begin to recognise the family implications and see that they are allowed for.

It should also, over the longer term, ask MPs and councillors to consult with local groups of churches, as suggested in the last chapter, to see what can be done which is socially desirable and legally feasible to bring back commitment to life-long marriage as a means to increase social stability and decrease the number of homeless children and dysfunctional partnerships.

The case for the Christian moral order

In dealing with this and other problems, where a slipping moral order has undermined our social structure, Government has to consider who else but the church has any track record of creating a supportive social structure. The church does not have an unblemished record over the long centuries in creating a stable moral order, but nor does government in creating a fair and stable social order.

Faced with the tidal wave of the permissive society, pornography, off the top shelf and easily accessible in every newsagent, access on the internet to even more debased views of women and children, violence on TV and video, politicians may well wonder what support remains for the nanny state. But tolerance cannot be endless. There must be a limit. The public outrage against paeodophiles has shown the resentment of parents whose children have to be escorted to and from school and have to spend their spare time indoors because it is no longer safe to play on the streets.

There is a tension too between the women's movements and the wide-spread treatment of women as mere sex objects for men's lust. Every breach of moral obligation creates its own enemies. Politicians know that final power is still with the people whom they canvass down side-streets, around suburban closes and up and down the stairs of blocks of flats.

Nor is the church so thin on the ground. Added to the active church members of 6.4 million, the sects' half a million and the minority religions 1.3 million, give a grand total of religious folk of 8.2 million, a good deal more than go to football matches and as high as the total membership of trades unions. These are tidy numbers and cannot be brushed aside.

The churches have been in decline, but this decline may soon level out. In the last five years which *Social Trends* record, they declined by just 1% a year. One's impression on going round the country is that the churches which have trimmed most to the secular position, together with the churches where religion is more of a social formality have been big losers, while the more active and committed churches are growing slowly to take their place, so the church has become leaner but much fitter and measured by the growth in its social work, much more active. Attendance at the four-day Easter conferences of the Evangelical churches in England and Wales is 70,000, which is far more than attend the annual conferences of all the political parties put together.

Add to that the 18% rise in the non-Christian religions, to which the family is also central and the number of those committed to the family by their religion has remained stable.

While secular humanism may dominate the heavyweight media and literature, it is not organised on the ground in Rotherham or Southend and it is most unlikely that it carries with it the proverbial patrons of the 'Dog and Duck,' who are stubbornly in favour of capital punishment for murder and whose views on race and on single-sex marriages are not politically correct. They are happy to take advantage of the permissive society, but it is its practice and not the theory which appeals to them. The country contains large sections of brutal backlash territory as any political canvasser would testify.

The church also has a secret weapon. It is the inner voice, which is known as conscience. It tells us all, often much against our will, what is right and what is wrong. Those who hear private confessions, whether clergy or psychiatrists, tell us that it is found even in the most hard-bitten. Those who make appeals for charity and ministers in the pulpit reach out to this conscience to stir it into life. We may not recognise the sins in ourselves, but as Paul pointed out to the Romans (Chapter 2), we are very quick to recognise them in others.

People may want to peep behind the bedroom door privately on TV, but when we find a politician in a compromising situation, most are quick to judge. Politicians, who thought that they lived in a society completely tolerant of sexual aberration, suddenly find that the door on their bright political future has banged shut forever and that there is no way round.

Despite the permissive society, a government which decided to encourage the family should expect a great deal of support and they should at least begin to test that support by giving a public lead.

Government is not just about legislation, it is also about leadership. We can dismiss political rhetoric as mere words. But words can capture the imagination. The older of us remember Churchill's 'fight them on the beaches,' Macmillan's 'winds of change' and Harold Wilson's 'white heat of technology.' All those speeches gave a vision, to rally the nation when we were on our knees, to make us realise that the days of Empire were over, to shift the fractious Labour party, a constructive goal. And, as the proverb says (Proverbs 29), 'Where there is no vision, the people perish.'

Good leadership encourages what is good in society.

Where to start

The lurch into the permissive society was not done from the grassroots up, it was done from the top down. I remember my Secretary of State, a great democrat, ribbing his Minister of State, who supported one of the more permissive bills then going through the Commons,

> Is your mailbag overflowing with letters from your constituents demanding this? I defy you to show me a single letter. Are they crowding into your surgery to insist on it? I doubt it. It is going through because you and your friends have decided that you're going to have it and the great British public have to lump it!

It is, however a great deal easier to tell people from the top down that they can do what they like than to replace the restraints which have been removed. In that work, I believe, for the government as well as the church a new partnership really has to start, city by city, from the bottom up.

We do not need a commission of the good and the great in the capital, we need the people directly involved to get together and to try to see what can best be done to help. Councillors and MPs will know who in the city is carrying their weight and ought to be heard and who are the doctrinaire wind-bags who can be safely ignored.

If government gets a positive response to its vision of a strong family underpinning our social order, it should ask MPs to consult locally with those who are in the thick of the problems and ask what can be done. Any new policy would then have the broadest possible foundation and be far more enduring than what is imposed on society from above.

Racism and Xenophobia

Finally there is an issue for government on which both Christians and humanists agree, and on which the church could and should be able to help.

Racism and Xenophobia come from the same stable. In one hatred is directed against fellow citizens, in the other, against foreigners. Both are defended on patriotic grounds. But, while we can see the effects of racism, it is only possible to see the impact of xenophobia from the countries at the receiving end.

It needs robust politicians to stand up against both racism and xenophobia. When Enoch Powell made his infamous 'rivers of blood speech,' he was dropped at once from the Conservative leadership and never returned.

Harold Macmillan, Alec Douglas Home and Edward Heath saw it as in our best interests to bring Britain into the close alliance of the European Community and even after two rebuffs by President de Gaulle, their speeches remained warm and friendly. But even though she had signed the Single European Act which pledged 'ever closer union', the next Conservative leader made a speech in Bruges three years later, which licensed Europhobia in the party and has divided it ever since.

There is no need to respond in kind. One of the most brilliant political speeches in our time was made by Helmut Schmidt, then Chancellor of Germany, to a Labour Party conference at a time when the Labour Party was especially hesitant about Europe. He spoke in perfect English and started by saying that, coming to a Labour Party conference to speak on Europe, he felt like a Salvation Army lass walking into a public house.

The very British image and his light and apologetic approach put the whole audience on his side and everyone listened as he said simply, 'We need you.'

I once persuaded the former French President, Valery Giscard d'Estaing to come to speak to my constituents in Cambridge. He told them,

> We two old nations understand each other. We both insist on keeping our national identity. I will always be a Frenchman and you will always be English. You would not want to change me and I would not want to change you. No one is going to take away our national identities.

As the audience looked at this personification of French elegance and charm, they could see that national identity was not up for grabs any-where. It was not the rest against the Brits. Europe was and always would be a partnership of nations.

The case against racism is nearer home. It is not simply a matter of black and white. As well as the Africans and Afro-Caribbeans, there are huge Irish and Asian minorities, each probably a million strong. There are substantial communities of Jews, Poles, Greek Cypriots and Chinese as well as smaller national groups. In my constituency, which was as English as they come, there were big Italian communities and both Bedford and Peterborough and I have a retirement present of two Cossack dancers from the Ukrainian community in Peterborough.

Racism is dangerous because, with sixty million people living together at high density, all heavily inter-dependent, we have no room to fall out with each other. The case against it should be spelt out with courage, skill and wit.

The Christian church is inherently multi-racial. As the Apostle John says repeatedly in the Book of Revelation, it is from 'every tribe, race, people and language,' and probably no more than one or two in a hun-dred are British. There are ten times as many practising Christians in Communist China as there are in Britain.

We should have laws against racial discrimination, but, as the Stephen Lawrence case showed, if there is racial bias in the arm of the law, the law alone is not enough. The Christian church, by its example, can and should do more than the arm of the law and should, as in Northern Ireland, South Africa and the Southern States of the USA, point out to churches which allow racial prejudice that they are in error. If for this cause alone, that government should learn to call on the aid of the church to help curb racism.

The urgent need for action

If nothing is done to stem the social collapse, then, one day, some unforeseen incident will trigger a backlash. At some level of unemployment, some depth of corruption of the nation's youth by drugs and decadence, too many people will have had enough and be tempted to take the law into their own hands. The mood in the 'Dog and Duck' will turn sour. Someone may organise the young unemployed into disciplined battalions, make them feel for the first time that they matter and give them something to live for, fight for and even die for. There is nothing much to chose between flag-carrying English football fans who smash the windows of French shop-keepers and the German brownshirts who smashed the windows of Jewish shopkeepers on Kristalnacht. They would support an overtly racist, nationalist party, flying the flag of St George, England for the English, drawing on the great battles of the past and as politically incorrect as it can be.

My old parliamentary colleague, Philip von Bismarck, once told me,

> We did not think that the Chancellor of Germany could be a gangster and, by the time we found out, it was too late.

After nearly half a century of peace in Northern Ireland, no one believed that 'the troubles' would ever come back again. The problem, thirty years on was that violence had its own momentum. Once started it becomes a way of life and is far harder to stop than to start. A democratically elected government should not take risks with democracy and the rule of law. It should put right what has gone wrong while it still has the power. The argument of this book is that it not only should be done, but that it can be done.

Appendix of Organisations

1. The Breakup of Families

Disorientated families

Save The Family — Plas Bellin (N Wales)

Drugs in the family

Yeldall Manor — Nr Reading
Adullam Homes — Nr Nottingham
Kickstart — Sheffield

Prisoners & their families

Prison fellowship — Northern Ireland

2. Loose cannons

Helping the schools

Stepping Stone Project — East Belfast
Ellen Wilkinson School — Manchester
Street Club — Manchester
Glasgow City Mission — Glasgow

Youth Projects

Romsey Mill — Cambridge
M13 Youth Project — Manchester

Teenage Pregnancy

Firgrove Centre — Southampton
LCET — Luton

Teenage Mothers

Drumchapel Emmaus Family Project — Glasgow
Orchard Family Centre — Peckham
Adullam Homes — Leicester

Living with AIDS

ACET — London, Brighton, Chichester, Northampton, South Wales, Clydeside, Tayside

The clutches of the law

United Evangelical Project — Aston & Handsworth

3. Homes for the homeless

Down and out

Friary Drop-In Centre	Nottingham
Bethany Christian Trust	Edinburgh

Covering the bare boards

Shaftesbury Resources Centre	Camberwell

Keeping the bailiff at bay

Bristol Debt Advice Centre	Bristol
Speakeasy Advice Centre	Roath, Cardiff

4. Jobs for the jobless

No one is unemployable

The Churches Trust	Londonderry
Rebuild	Sheffield
SENTA	Sheffield
Priority 5	Sheffield

Finding jobs

PECAN	Peckham

5. Churches in the community

The Bridge Chapel	Garston, Liverpool
West Street Baptist Church	Crewe
King's Centre	Chessington

6. City Networks

Nottingham
Hackney
Southampton

For further information about any of these projects or Christian Action Networks please contact the Evangelical Alliance at:
Whitefield House
186 Kennington Park Road
London
SE11 4BT

Tel: 0207 207 2100
e-mail: **cans@eauk.org**   website: **www.eauk.org**